EDITOR IN CHIEF:.....................................PAMELA USCHUK
POETRY EDITOR...............................WILLIAM PITT ROOT
GUEST POETRY EDITOR:.......................PAMELA USCHUK
FICTION EDITOR....................................BETH ALVARADO
GUEST FICTION EDITOR:............LUIS ALBERTO URREA
ONLINE FICTION EDITOR:...................WILLIAM LUVAAS
MANAGING EDITOR...................................SUSAN FOSTER
ASSISTANT FICTION EDITORS:........TAWNYSHA GREEN
                                                        ALISON MCCABE
ASSISTANT POETRY EDITOR:...........HOWIE FAERSTEIN
DESIGN EDITOR:........................ALEXANDRA COGSWELL
EDITORIAL ASSISTANT INTERN:......GABRIELA FLORES

CONTRIBUTING EDITORS: Sandra Alcosser, Charles Baxter, Frank Bergon, Red Bird, Janet Burroway, Robert Olen Butler, Ram Devineni, Elizabeth Dewberry, Rick DeMarinis, Joy Harjo, Richard Jackson, Marilyn Kallet, Richard Katrovas, Zelda Lockhart, Demetria Martinez, John McNally, Jane Mead, Penelope Niven, Dennis Sampson, Rebecca Seiferle, and Lyrae vanClief-Stefanon.

Send submissions, subscription payments and inquiries to:
Cutthroat, A Journal of the Arts
P.O. Box 2124,
Durango, Colorado 81302.

ph: 970-903-7914
email: cutthroatmag@gmail.com

Make checks payable to:
Raven's Word Writers Center or Cutthroat, A Journal of the ArtS

Subscriptions are $25 per two issues or $15 for a single issue.
We are self-funded so all Donations gratefully accepted.

CUTTHROAT

2015 JOY HARJO POETRY PRIZE
RICK DEMARINIS SHORT STORY PRIZE

$1250 1st Prize, $250 2nd Prize, Honorable Mention

JUDGES
NATALIE DIAZ, POETRY
TBA, SHORT STORY
NICK FLYNN, CREATIVE NONFICTION

GUIDELINES: Go to www.cutthroatmag.com and submit poems and stories through our online submission manager or submit through the mail. Include SASE for announcement of winners is REQUIRED for all mailed entries. Submit up to 3 poems (100 line limit/one poem per page) or one short story or creative nonfiction piece (5000 word limit/double s spaced) in 12 point font. NO AUTHOR NAME ALLOWED ON ANY MS. Mail-ins must have a cover sheet with author name, address, phone & email, title(s) of submission, SASE for announcement of winners (all mss. recycled). There is a $18 nonrefundable entry fee per submission. Make checks to Ravens Word Writers. Deadline: October 20, 2015. UNPUBLISHED WORK ONLY! No work that has already won a prize is eligible. No former CUTTHROAT prize-winning author may enter the contest he/or she has previously won. Enter as often as you wish. Multiple submissions okay, but we must be informed immediately of acceptances elsewhere. Finalists considered for publication. Winners published in CUTTHROAT and announced on our website, in POETS & WRITERS and AWP CHRONICLE. No relatives of or staff members of CUTTHROAT nor close friends, relatives and no students of judges are eligible to enter our contests. See www.cutthroatmag.com for more information. WE RECOMMEND YOU READ A COPY OF CUTTHROAT BEFORE ENTERING OUR CONTESTS.

CUTTHROAT THANKS

WEBSITE DESIGN:...........................LAURA PRENDERGAST
PAMELA USCHUK

COVER LAYOUT:...........................ALEXANDRA COGSWELL
PAMELA USCHUK

MAGAZINE LAYOUT:..................ALEXANDRA COGSWELL
PAMELA USCHUK

LOGO DESIGN:............................LYNN MCFADDEN WATT

FRONT COVER ART:.............................ANITA ENDREZZE
Koi, acylic on canvas

BACK COVER ART:..................................ANITA ENDREZZE
Salmon, Colored pencil sketch

AND THANK YOU TO:

CONTEST JUDGES: Martín Espada and Bobbie Ann Mason

CONTEST READERS: Beth Alvarado, Howie Faerstein, Tim Rien, William Pitt Root, J. Stahl, Ken Stahl, and Pamela Uschuk.

Alexandra Cogswell for her expertise in setting up the magazine and the cover. Gabriela Flores, Alexandra Cogswell and Susan Foster for their help with proofreading and editorial assistance.

Thank you to all writers who submitted to Cutthroat and to our literary contests. We value every single piece of work that is submitted. We also thank our subscribers around the world.

CUTTHROAT

THE CUTTHROAT ONLINE WRITING MENTOR PROGRAM

ONE-ON-ONE, FOUR WEEK MENTORSHIPS IN POETRY, MEMOIR, MIXED GENRE, NOVEL, POETRY, SHORT STORY AND POETRY IN TRANSLATION ($1000). WE ALSO OFFER SIX WEEK MANUSCRIPT EVALUATION OF POETRY COLLECTIONS, NOVELS, SCREENPLAYS AND SHORT STORY COLLECTIONS ($2000).

FACULTY
DOUG ANDERSON, Poetry and Memoir
BETH ALVARADO, Memoir And Short Story
STEVE BARANCIK, Screenwriting
SEAN THOMAS DOUGHERTY, Mixed Genre
ANNIE FINCH, Poetry
JOY HARJO, Memoir And Poetry
LINDA HOGAN, Personal Essays
PATRICIA SPEARS JONES, Poetry
LORIAN HEMINGWAY, Short Story
RICHARD JACKSON, Poetry and Poetry in Translation
MARILYN KALLET, Manuscript Evaluation Only (Poetry And Poetry In Translation)
WILLIAM LUVAAS, Short Story
DARLIN NEAL, Flash Fiction/Short Story
MEG POKRASS, Flash Fiction
MELISSA PRITCHARD, Short Story
WILLIAM PITT ROOT, Poetry
PATRICIA SMITH, Poetry
PAMELA USCHUK, Poetry
DONLEY WATT, The Novel

INFORMATION
Go to www.cutthroatmag.com or call 970-903-7914 for complete guidelines, fee schedules and enrollment information.

CONGRATULATIONS TO THE WINNERS OF OUR 2014 LITERARY AWARDS

Congratulations to the winners of the 2014 Rick DeMarinis Short Story Award chosen by Bobbie Ann Mason:

First Prize ($1250)
Aleksey Babyev of New York City for "Top Of The Morning"

Second Prize ($250)
Jacob Appel of New York City for "Thorns For The Negro."

Honorable Mention (Publication)
Mason Boyles of Wilmington, North Carolina, "Erosion."

Congratulations to the winners of the 2014 Joy Harjo Poetry Prizes chosen by Martin Espada:

First Prize ($1250)
Terri Kirby Erickson of Lewisville, North Carolina for "After The Explosion"

Second Prize ($250 plus)
Chen Chen of Syracuse, New York for, "First Light"

Honorable Mention (Publication)
Hope Maxwell Snyder of Columbia and now living in West Virginia, for "Blue Nights."

2014 RICK DEMARINIS SHORT STORY AWARD FINALISTS

Sharon Solwitz, *Camp Happiness*
Leslie Johnson, *Cookie Time*
Lorriane Ridley, *The Hell Child*
Kate Hanson, *Ascension*
Emily Doak, *The End of a Generation*
Cady Vishniac, *Coyote In The Manger*
Jacob Appel, *Thieving In A Minor Key* and *The Prophet of Heathridge Hills*
Celine Keating, *Home*
Terrance Manning Jr., *Crick*
Milena Nigam, *Seville*
Anne Holbrook, *Northern Straits*
Michele Anderson, *Cancer & Other Curses*
Stephen Cahill, *The DNR Protocol*
Erik Sakariassen, *Starlight, Moonlight*

2014 JOY HARJO POETRY AWARD FINALISTS

Whitney Vale, *At the Retreat the Urge of Voice*
Sylvia Baumgartel, *Juarez*
Tony Barnstone, *River Eels*
Alexander Long, *I am Also Going to Speak of Hope*
Stuart Freyer, *Following His Tracks*
Abbey Murray, *Lunch at the War College*
Barbara Tran, *Unframed*
Marc Jampole, *Song Jiang Spares the Geese*
Janlori Goldman, *Nablus, 2012*
Esteban Ismael, *Dixie Cup Psalm*
Alysia Harris, *When I Look At You Without Speaking I'm Drawing A Map*
Nadia Chaney, *Wintering Place*
Tom Wayman, *Blue North*
Judith Ferster, *Zion in the Ganglia*
Dean Ellis, *Plum/ Holocaust*
Dexter Booth, *The Retreat at Twin Lakes*
Ellen La Fleche, *Sitting by my window during a snowstorm, three months after becoming a widow*
Deborah Doolittle, *Paradigms*

Table of Contents

Joy Harjo Poetry Prize

Prose

Rick DeMarinis Short Story Prize

2015 Lorian Hemingway Short Story Winner

Fiction

Introduction

As an introduction to this collection of poetry, short stories and creative nonfiction, honoring Linda Hogan and Joy Harjo, two of America's finest women writers, Luis Alberto Urrea and I decided we would write two rememberances of them. Luis was Linda's student at the University of Colorado, Boulder, and I was Joy Harjo's student at the University of Montana. Luis and I have worked over a year to assemble this collection, bursting with powerful work. This was orignally Luis's idea, one that I immediately embraced. It is a true labor of love. We dedicate this to Joy and Linda, a gift to them for sharing so much grace with us.

~Pam Uschuk, March 2015

LINDA HOGAN, A REMEMBRANCE BY LUIS ALBERTO URREA

After my first book had been rejected steadily for ten years, I skulked off to grad school. I thought I was not fated to make it as a writer, and CU Boulder had Linda Hogan on its faculty. She, and Lorna Dee Cervantes and Vine Deloria were the magnets that pulled me into the Rockies. More than a teacher, Linda became a mentor and a friend. She and Lorna presided over Sherman Alexie's visit--we were both long haired boys (though I was faking it--I was already old) and felt like we were kicking off our careers in my Jeep.

Linda and I somehow began eating salmon fish and chips at a local brewery, and I learned more from her in those lunches than I did anywhere but her books. "The human body," she told me, "is a sovereign nation." It was Linda who first listened to the entire life story of Teresita (The Hummingbird's Daughter). I had been collecting data and stories for six years by then, and I sat in her office and narrated all I knew for two long hours. Then I tried to talk her into writing it.

"Why me?" she asked.

"It's a woman's story," I said.

"But she's your aunt. She's your woman. It's your duty, not mine."

"But," I argued, "it's an indigenous story."

She said, "Study."

I cried, "But my western mind can't grasp these Indian stories."

She said two things to me that stay with me. I give them to you. First: "Remember who you were in Mexico. Remember what you knew and forgot." And the one that still brings the house down at readings: "Honey, the western mind is a fever. It will pass." It will pass. I am happy to report that we have remained friends, though life drags people apart. But, like some crazy twister, suddenly throws them back together again. Last year, I was lucky enough to hang out with her in North Carolina. My family and I drove her up to Cherokee, to see what was going on and to visit the tribal museum. You haven't lived till you've seen Linda holler to Cherokee dancers in full regalia, "Where's the buffalo burgers?" A singular talent, a great wisdom, a greater joy.

JOY HARJO REMEMBRANCE BY PAM USCHUK

During a rough Missoula winter, snow blowing wild through everyone's souls, shifting the patterns of highways, making traction tricky, I was finishing up my final year of graduate school, and to pay for that, I drove back and forth across black-iced Montana roads, teaching poetry on reservation schools, working with kindergarten through 12 grade Indian students, staying in cheap motels, rushing back to campus for classes.

I volunteered to pick up Joy Harjo, our first Richard Hugo Visiting Poet, from the airport. Jim Welch told me that she was really something, cocking his head, half closing his brown eyes and smiling, a look and tone of voice he reserved for people he admired.

When that small plane landed, a Chinook wind blew in a tall, slim thaw with long black hair, eyes so ancient that I was struck deep, and a voice lyrical with laughter and resonant with gravitas I knew as wisdom. On the way to her motel, we stopped at the Clark Fork River so she could breathe in water's wild and clear intent. She talked to me as if I was an old friend. From the first day she walked into my life, shooting stars, yellow balsa root, and delicate pasque flowers sprouted up through the drifts, and the Hellgate wind stopped blowing so hard.

There are moments that change everything, and your life that has wobbled, leaning over the lip of despair, suddenly brightens, and you know that if you step out in the fearful air, you will fly.

Joy turned out to be one of the finest teachers I had at University of Montana. She introduced us to writers of color outside the canon, like June Jordan, Audre Lorde, Ishmael Reed, Sandra Cisneros, and Native poets such as Leslie Silko, Linda Hogan and Adrian Louis, who awakened us to voices speaking out against social injustices. No one missed class. Why would we? No one, including me, wanted to miss a word she said. We were graced with an oracle, a female Crazy Horse, a visionary poet-teacher, surely with feet of clay like the rest of us, but she never denied that, which made us love her even more. Quickly she won us over with candor, with music, with love. Never arrogant of self-serving, she taught us that "poets are truth-tellers," that "we must turn slaughter into food." We felt like lost relatives sitting around her kitchen table. She taught us to risk everything, to create images that bridged the real and the spirit worlds, using deep music to preserve the stories of our ancestors, to preserve the magic and mystery in our own work. I learned valuable teaching tools, to walk as an equal with my students, as she would say, "this journey for all of us…"

Thus began our long friendship. Despite great distances and changing relationships, Joy and I are still in frequent and close contact. Joy and I read and criticize each other's work. She is one of the major gifts of my life.

Joy Harjo

Conflict Resolution For Holy Beings

"I am the holy being of my mother's prayer and my father's song"
Norman Patrick Brown, Dineh poet and speaker

1. Set conflict resolution ground rules:

Recognize whose lands these are on which we stand.
Ask the deer, turtle, and the crane.
Make sure the spirits of these lands are respected and treated with good will.
The land is a being who remembers everything.
You will have to answer to your children, and their children, and theirs--
The red shimmer of remembering will compel you up the night to walk the perimeter
of truth for understanding.
As I brushed my hair over the hotel sink to get ready I heard:
By listening we will understand who we are in this holy realm of words.
Do not parade, pleased with yourself.
You must speak in the language of justice.

2. Use effective communication skills that display and enhance mutual trust and respect:

If you sign this paper we will become brothers. We will no longer fight. We will give you
this land and these waters "as long as the grass shall grow and the rivers run".

The lands and waters they gave us did not belong to them to give. Under false
pretenses we signed. After drugging by drink, we signed. With a mass of gun power
pointed at us, we signed. With a flotilla of war ships at our shores, we signed. We are
still signing. We have found no peace in this act of signing.

A casino was raised up over the gravesite of our ancestors. Our own distant cousins
pulled up the bones of grandparents, parents and grandchildren from their last
sleeping place. They had forgotten how to be human beings. Restless winds emerged
from the earth when the graves were open and the winds went looking for justice.

If you raise this white flag of peace, we will honor it.

At Sand Creek several hundred women, children and men were slaughtered in an unspeakable massacre, after a white flag was raised. The American soldiers trampled the white flag in the blood of the peacemakers.

There is a suicide epidemic among native children. It is triple the rate of the rest of America. "It feels like wartime," said a child welfare worker in South Dakota.

If you send your children to our schools we will train them to get along in this changing world. We will educate them.

We had no choice. They took our children. Some ran away and froze to death. If they were found they were dragged back to the school and punished. They cut their hair, took away their language, until they became as strangers to themselves even as they became strangers to us.

If you sign this paper we will become brothers. We will no longer fight. We will give you this land and these waters in exchange "as long as the grass shall grow and the rivers run."

Put your hand on this bible, this blade, this pen, this oil derrick, this gun and you will gain trust and respect with us. Now we can speak together as one.

We say, put down your papers, your tools of coercion, your false promises, your posture of superiority and sit with us before the fire. We will share food, songs and stories. We will gather beneath starlight and dance, and rise together at sunrise.

The sun rose over the Potomac this morning, over the city surrounding the white house.
It blazed scarlet, a fire opening truth.
White House, or *Chogo Hvtke* means the house of the peacekeeper, the keepers of justice.
We have crossed this river to speak to the white leader for peace many times
Since these settlers first arrived in our territory and made this their place of governance.
These streets are our old trails, curved to fit around trees.

3. Give constructive feedback:

We speak together with this trade language of English. This trade language enables us to speak across many language boundaries. These languages have given us the poets:

Ortiz, Silko, Momaday, Alexie, Diaz, Bird, Woody, Kane, Bitsui, Long Soldier, White, Erdrich, Tapahonso, Howe, Louis, Brings Plenty, Okpik, Hill, Wood, Maracle, Cisneros, Trask, Hogan, Dunn, Welch…

The 1957 Chevy is unbeatable in style. My broken down one-eyed Ford will have to do. It holds everyone: Grandma and grandpa, aunties and uncles, the children and the babies, and all my boyfriends. That's what she said, anyway, as she drove off for the Forty-Nine with all of us in that shimmying wreck.

This would be no place to be without blues, jazz—Thank you/*mvto* to the Africans, the Europeans sitting in, especially Adolfe Sax with his saxophones... Don't forget that at the center is the Mvskoke ceremonial circles. We know how to swing. We keep the heartbeat of the earth in our stomp dance feet.

You might try dancing theory with a bustle, or a jingle dress, or with turtles strapped around your legs. You might try wearing colonization like a heavy gold chain around a pimp's neck.

4. Reduce defensiveness and break the defensiveness chain:

I could hear the light beings as they entered every cell. Every cell is a house of the god of light they said. I could hear the spirits who love us stomp dancing. They were dancing as if they were here, and then another level of here, and then another, until the whole earth and sky was dancing.

We are here dancing, they said. There was no there.

There was no "I" or "you".

There was us; there was "we".

There we were as if we were the music.

You cannot legislate music to lock step nor can you legislate the spirit of the music to stop at political boundaries—

--Or poetry, or art, or anything that is of value or matters in this world, and the next worlds.

This is about getting to know each other.

We will wind up back at the blues standing on the edge of the flatted fifth about to jump into a fierce understanding together.

5. Eliminate negative attitudes during conflict:

A panther poised in the cypress tree about to jump is a panther poised in a cypress tree about to jump.

The panther is a poem of fire green eyes and a heart charged by four winds of four directions.

The panther hears everything in the dark: the unspoken tears of a few hundred human years, storms that will break what has broken his world, a bluebird swaying on a branch a few miles away.

He hears the death song of his approaching prey:

I will always love you sunrise.
I belong to the black cat with fire green eyes.
There, in the cypress tree near the morning star.

6. And, use what you learn to resolve your own conflicts and to mediate others conflicts:

When we made it back home, back over those curved roads that wind through the city of peace, we stopped at the doorway of dusk as it opened to our homelands. We gave thanks for the story, for all parts of the story because it was by the light of those challenges we knew ourselves—
We asked for forgiveness.
We laid down our burdens next to each other.

From Joy Harjo's CONFLICT RESOLUTION FOR HOLY BEINGS, W.W. Norton,
Fall 2015

Linda Hogan

Burying the Horse

She came to me
mere bone
dark,
blood in hooves,
barely able
to move or eat
without help.
All the way home
she watched me
behind the trailer
and that was a
beginning
of what would become
the long black hair
in the wind,
the looking back to see
that I was
still there,
my own hair black then
blowing as I leaned out
so she could see.

In time
she grew red
and larger,
and turned out
to be an Arabian.
One day
I saw her healthy,
running like wind
was pushing her along
its currents.

For all the years after,
she was grateful for every morsel
of food and for grass.
How she loved it,
and the dog
pretending to be a horse
out in the field bent over
as if eating beside her.

She was the one not to ride
because she'd been so abused
nothing could make her turn
from grass
or walk on.
Nothing.

And so the years went,
senior feed,
medicine,
love. To all she showed
such gratitude
and care returning
kindness,
even her eyes showed it
the happy fragility,

and even that same look
when I stayed
with her head in my lap
as she was dying.
I held the red umbrella
over her
from the Oklahoma
summer heat
as we waited
four hours for the death-maker

to arrive
and put her down
then leave me in the chosen place
with her lifeless body
while her sister
studied her
and understood
she was gone
and she was alone,

and the living one stayed
while I waited
for the backhoe
to arrive then
to dig a hole
and I wrapped her
in more than my arms,
in an Indian blanket
and began trying to get her down
that hole,
but a horse is so heavy
and I bent and pushed
with a friend and his one good arm,
and felt wretched,
as I saw how she finally landed
not the way I wanted
with her dignity
and fragile beauty
but fell into the
consuming hole
which would swallow
her any way it wanted.

Oh my love
how it hurt my body so
but even more my heart

to get you down there
with so little of the help
you'd always given me
just to see you eat
with such untethered happiness
and to see you run
across fields with wild
freedom,
to have watched you heal
from bones to belly
and part of me
is beneath that ground
in the blanket
wrapped and singing
a good horse song
the horse song
the horse song.
Each nation has them,
even the nation
of horses.

Linda Hogan

On Kindness

When all else is gone
only kindness will do.

When a child becomes an animal in clouds
changing forms to other creatures
it is kindness to the sky.

When the hay is rolled and you think what if
there was a mouse or snake inside,
that is a gentle question to think.

When the horses are fed and all that's left is a withered apple
for a woman to eat and she is grateful
            for the life of all things
that is a good heart.

When you are gentle to the skin of others,
touching them so softly, that is compassion.

When there is agreement,
it is a gift to all.

If skin is the first organ to form in the body of woman
that is kindness and a mother's first protection.

If you still love the invisible place of a standing child,
that is kindness.

And when you pick up the old woman on the
reservation road and take her home and inside
she has nothing, you give her all the food you have,
the can of coffee, and start her woodstove,
then leave your coat, that is what a human
being must do.

And gathering roots and berries
to feed the others, I am thinking only kindness,
finding medicine plants for the sick.

I know there is a nursery of stars
out in the universe, infant stars. The future
may see their light when they grow
as you see the kind light of the old ones
now here.

Linda Hogan
The Night In Turkey

I forget too many things
but I will never forget the dancers
in the stone church out far in the country.
It was night. The milk in the cold sky
was strongly drawn.
Inside we sat with tea
and the men came out,
nodded at one another, just men
in white robes
and it seems music began
but that I can barely remember
because the men began encircling themselves
at the very core of life
and whirling, stepped in together,
their robes opening out
like tender flowers in first spring.

It seemed the sky unfurled
in all its starlit splendor,
one white moon in the darkness
after another
and the world began to bloom warm again.
The human all had vanished
as we were entranced
and nothing in this world could have missed it.

All this, all this, because something in the human
was silenced and dancers opened in their life
to something greater in the darkness
and we were there with them,
as we became one of them
in a world that bloomed one winter night
from inside a dark building of stone
that fell away from all of us.

Linda Hogan

Dear Pablo,

In truth
what is an ode,?
I'm sorry I had no real education.
At first I thought the odes were praise to beauty,
the orange cathedral,
the lemon, your own suit in your body shape, but empty.
Then came the bomb you wrote about
and was that a praise,
that tiny atom on your thumbnail,
to what can be thrown away by the mere task of one
and ash of another.

I know there is a door between the worlds
and I need you and the other teachers
to whisper through it
to tell me these things
before I am such a fool.

But I am a fool who knows the earth,
the shining strands beneath the ground,
the plants and power of the black walnut trees
stolen from my family
cut during war for gunstock.
One man
thought I lied
but I haven't learned yet
to make a poem lie
and perhaps I need to know this.

I know the rattlesnakes here
and the garden snakes,
their very beauty,
and that the bulbs need taken apart.
I see how water willows downhill
all lie down in obedience to the flood,

though other trees landed
against thicker ones.
It's not as safe there as poison ivy
which must love me because I pull on its long roots,
stems and leaves with bare hands
and safety.

I go scratched through brambles
just to write the truth
so please don't let me down
because the world and her people everywhere
break me and put me together
with their war and love.
All I ask is that my words say all this
and carry some beauty, some soul, some heart
but no words that sound
like I am a fool
clumsy with truth,
only a bit of the moon,
a trembling seismic voice,
a tiny moon with a rainbow at night
encircling
and it's also what this fool wants to do
to end such thirst, such hunger,
empty of all but words
and truth
until I am only bone or
as I wish, ash
in my loved earth
and her people,
flying encircled.

Martín Espada

Haunt Me

For My Father

I am the archeologist. I sift the shards of you: cufflinks, passport photos,
a button from the March on Washington with a black hand shaking
a white hand, letters in Spanish, your birth certificate from a town high
in the mountains. I cup your silence, and the silence melts like ice in a cup.

I search for you in two yellow Kodak boxes marked *Puerto Rico,*
Noche Buena, Diciembre 1968. In the 8-millimeter silence the Espadas
gather, elders born before the Spanish American War, my grandfather
on crutches after fracturing his fossil hip, his blind brother on a cane.
You greet the elders and they call you *Tato,* the name they call you here.
Uncles and cousins sing in a chorus of tongues without sound, vibration
of guitar strings stilled by an unseen hand, maracas shaking empty
of seeds. The camera wobbles from the singers to the television
and the astronauts sending pictures of the moon back to earth.
Down by the river, women still pound laundry on the rocks.

I am eleven again, a boy from the faraway city of ice that felled
my grandfather, startled after the blind man with the cane stroked
my face with his hand dry as straw, crying out *Bendito.* At the table,
I hear only the silence that rises like the river in my big ears.
You sit next to me, clowning for the camera, tugging the lapels
on your jacket, slicking back your black hair, brown skin darker
from days in the sun. You slide your arm around my shoulder,
your good right arm, your pitching arm, and my moon face radiates,
and the mountain song of my uncles and cousins plays in my head.

Watching you now, my face stings as it stung when my blind great-uncle
brushed my cheekbones, searching for his own face. When you died,
Tato, I took a razor to the movie looping in my head, cutting the scenes
where you curled an arm around my shoulder, all the times you would
squeeze the silence out of me so I could hear the cries and songs again.
When you died, I heard only the silences between us, the shouts belling
the air before the phone went dead, all the words melting like ice in a cup.
That way I could set my jaw and take my mother's hand at the mortuary,
greet the elders in my suit and tie at the memorial, say all the right words.

Yet, my face stings at last. I rewind and watch your arm drape across
my shoulder, over and over. A year ago, you pressed a Kodak slide
of my grandfather into my hand and said: *Next time, stay longer.*
Now, in the silence that is never silent, I push the chair away
from the table and say to you: *Sit down. Tell me everything. Haunt me.*

Rita Dove

Insomnia Etiquette

There's a movie on, so I watch it.

The usual white people
in love, distress. The usual tears.
Good camera work, though:
sunshine waxing the freckled curves
of a pear, a clenched jaw —
more tragedy, then.

I get up for some Scotch and Stilton.
I don't turn on the lights.
I like moving through the dark
while the world sleeps on,
serene as a stealth bomber
nosing through clouds . . .

call it a preemptive strike,
"a precautionary measure
so sadly necessary in these perilous times".
I don't call it anything
but greediness: the weird glee
of finding my way without incident.

I know tomorrow I will regret
having the Stilton. I will regret
not being able to find
a book to get lost in,
and all those years I could get lost
in anything. Until then

it's just me and you,
Brother Night — moonless,
plunked down behind enemy lines
with no maps, no matches.
The woods deep.
Cheers.

First published in *Slate*.

Sandra Cisneros

Canto For Women of a Certain Llanto

after Dylan Thomas

I'd rather wear none
than ugly underwear made
for women of a certain age.

Rage, rage. Do not go into that good night
wearing sensible white or beige.

Women who have squash-
blossomed into soft flesh,
and grieve the frothy loss of the interior
garments of youth.

Rage, rage. Do not go into that good night
wearing sensible white or beige.

Gone the black-lace architecture of the past,
the thong, bikinis, hipsters, g-strings. Gone, gone.

The underwire and lace push-up cups
replaced with feed sacks and ace
bandage straps. Pachydermian.
Prosthetic. A cruel aesthetics.

Rage, rage. Do not go into that good night
wearing sensible white or beige.

Excellent women, who in wise vision flower,
Blaze, scintillate in your finest era.
Refuse the misnomer "Intimate Apparel."
For what lies beyond XL or 36C is
the antithesis of intimacy.
Garments sent to *exile ánimas solas*

to the Siberia of celibacy.
To sleep with dogs or cats
instead of lovers.

Oh, La Perla, why hast thou forsaken us?
Will no one take pity and design foundations, nay,
lingerie for women of exuberance?
Something imaginative, like Frank
Lloyd Wright's "Falling Water."

In my imagination I create
a holster to pack my twin firearms.
My 38-38's. A beautiful invention of oiled
Italian leather graced tobacco golden,
whip-stitched, hand tooled with western
roses and winged scrolls,
mother-of-pearl snaps and nipples
capped with silver aureoles.

And you, my mother, gazing from your sorry height,
who has cursed and blessed me with your DNA
like so many Mexican women
with a pillar for a torso
like Coatlicue.

Magas, brujas, chingonas.
Rage, rage. Do not go into that good night
wearing sensible white or beige.

Carolyn Forché

The Museum
of Stones

These are your stones, assembled in matchbox and tin,
collected from roadside, culvert and viaduct,
battlefield, threshing floor, basilica, abattoir—
stones, loosened by tanks in the streets
from a city whose earliest map was drawn in ink on linen,
schoolyard stones in the hand of a corpse,
pebble from Baudelaire's *oui*,
stone of the mind within us
carried from one silence to another
stone of cromlech and cairn, schist and shale, horneblende,
agate, marble, millstones, ruins of choirs and shipyards,
chalk, marl, mudstone from temples and tombs,
stone from the silvery grass near the scaffold,
stone from the tunnel lined with bones,
lava of a city's entombment, stones
chipped from lighthouse, cell wall, scriptorium,
paving stones from the hands of those who rose against the army,
stones where the bells had fallen, where the bridges were blown,
those that had flown through windows, weighted petitions,
feldspar, rose quartz, blueschist, gneiss and chert,
fragments of an abbey at dusk, sandstone toe
of a Buddha mortared at Bamiyan,
stone from the hill of three crosses and a crypt,
from a chimney where storks cried like human children,
stones newly fallen from stars, a stillness of stones, a heart,
altar and boundary stone, marker and vessel, first cast, load and hail,
bridge stones and others to pave and shut up with,
stone apple, stone basil, beech, berry, stone brake,
      stone bramble, stone fern, lichen, liverwort, pippin and root,

concretion of the body, as blind as cold as deaf,
all earth a quarry, all life a labor, stone-faced, stone-drunk
with hope that this assemblage of rubble, taken together, would become
a shrine or holy place, an ossuary, immoveable and sacred
like the stone that marked the path of the sun as it entered the human dawn.

First appeared in The New Yorker

Carolyn Forché

Morning on the Island

The lights across the water are the waking city.
The water shimmers with imaginary fish.
Not far from here lie the bones of conifers
washed from the sea and piled by wind.
Some mornings I walk upon them,
bone to bone, as far as the lighthouse.
A strange beetle has eaten most of the trees.
It may have come here on the ships playing
music in the harbor, or it was always here, a winged
jewel, but in the past was kept still by the cold
of a winter that no longer comes.
There is an owl living in the firs behind us but he is white,
meant to be mistaken for snow burdening a bough.
They say he is the only owl remaining. I hear him at night
listening for the last of the mice and asking *who* of no other owl.

first appeared in *The Nation*

Sherwin Bitsui

Exerpt from
DISSOLVE

A bottom lit sea
ponders the lake's questions,
their secret conversations
thatch howls to whimpers

exhaled from an isthmus of drowned wolves.

Its glossary's cataclysms,
smoothed over the hatchet
tucked into a sheath of starlight,
        locates fractures potted in cisterns of smog.

The stitching then unthreads
to muzzled worms pulsing,
        where an arson
        begins to lather heat over his neck.

Back-lit by a caravan of wailing fathers,
he silences their smeared faces
while kneeling over fire tipped spears
        in an arbor of mesh and steel.

        Nowhere streams in blips and beeps under them.

Michael Wasson

Cleansing

His skull is leaking
Our kitchen   a shoreline
for a thick red river

for hot springs   steam
for a body returning
home   dragging itself

She struggles
to hold   his head
in place

*

Puncture weed   upright nails
A bright buck knife in my soft hand
gutting my first deer
don't break
the belly bag
don't stink up the whole damn place

Always remember to
throw out dem remains   for
the coyotes

*

The blood dries in mom's fingernails
She works with holding his emptying head
her other hand pads with rags

unbalanced   the neck bone twists
back and forth   like a pail of water
my mom carries into a plume of smoke

Her arms tire   the blood drains
from her right   she tells me

Hold this 'n take the rag
take this fuckin rag
go 'n git me another one

        *

I shot the deer
square in the forehead
I cupped its heart all the way back home
it beat warm in my hands
like a chest I've pressed my ear against

Looking at its dark flesh
aware of a blurring landscape
around me I felt the cool air
licking the edges of my palms
a naked heart's skin exposed

We ate heart soup and marrow
that night   The sound now
as often   as my body's
own throb.

        *

My brother sucks on the copper shell
not crying

Bullets are binkies
on the reservation

taste like money
in the mouth.

Michael Wasson

American Reservation

I'm to leave the reservation soon, to go reduce into the small cities
maybe far into foreign lands of rising suns and islanded tongues.
This garden here I watched re-grow and re-wilt over the years
has always looked to me as though bitter gourds blossoming
splayed barrels like slow buds opening outward, switch knives
curling out from around the thin stems, the breath of an uncle
with his hardy, hairy arm around me. That smile.

Our American ghosts still drag their shackled feet around
still wear their hair untied, still watch uncle get tired of burning
his hair in mourning every year, keeping him from dancing the powwows
all chopped up and rugged looking ever since
he's had those dreams of burying my little cousin in the crushed
purple powwow van and grandma's tender still-barely-kickin' body
locked around such knocked flesh. You should've seen his bloody hands.

My uncle stays up tonight to talk about grizzly bears,
lost visions, starving too long in the mountains, diner signs of *No Dogs
or Indians Allowed*, telling me about when my mother was threatened
because her redskin trash was no good for customers. He'd even get all
riled up about politics, about constitutional law, 12 Stat. 957,
keeping our treaty papers in the glove box for when cops want to profile us.
Good ol' northwest he'd say. *Same ol' rez, ennit.*

Sitting with him, the fire crackling, the black and white photos
all over the walls, the medallions, the purple heart, the dim bottle of whiskey
the smile of his family members in a photo now wiped out of these dirty rooms
those two rooms in this bright dark he says, *blinding almost* he says
the stacked laundry, the sticky jam spots here and there on the floor
the room he leaves his light on, and that La-Z-Boy. That La-Z-Boy in this living room
he rocks on and never cries even when death or sasquatch
or whatever witch knocks down his garbage cans, and he sits not eating.

The chicken dancing he did when he was dancing the trail
the babies he'd wanted to grow from beautiful women

the baby he'd grow and lose on an icy road
that young face peeled off, my grandma's broken body holding dead-tight
and uncle just getting out, stumbling there hollering his pain
his grief the sound of his boots dragging the ground
his hunched over body until some family brought him home
and unbraided his fuzzy hair, his to-be knife-wrecked braids and ponytails.
It's all that blood deep in the winter
all those lost in the war of home tangling up his knotted hair
all the opened bodies that ripple and crack the curbs
right along the bar, the gas station, the school.

Before I leave him and hear the woodchips fall from his red flannel
before he takes another breather to *tu'x* up
he adjusts his mouth and takes my hand in his
them hands that could snap deer knees and gut better than any surgeon
and says *we don't die here, neph. Come back alive at least one more time.*

I pretend I'm not afraid and give him a hug.
I unlock the front door, step out and stand close by.
His dry field near the border of the rez where some young men
were found this morning as uncle was waking me up.
They were dragged through the field. People called them faggots
left them there, the rope still cut into their legs.
Their footsteps broke somewhere past the ravine, those trails of running lives
the screen door behind me rattling shut.

— for runaways, for homebodies

Anita Endrezze

The Secret of Black

There's the kettle, its anger against the pot
sputtering with sizzling spit upon the rim.
And the pot which calls itself
dainty, filling itself with lies of honey
or tea, damp leaves that tell the future
of bitter secret quarrels.

There's the cat, with its twitching tail,
defining darkness with her whiskers. She arches
her back, sleek fur shining
like rippling night. Black
is every paw fall, each step quick on the curious
earth. And in her dreams, black curves
 its wicked claws over the humped- back rat,
 or a dark bird that quivers weakly.

Black is all colors combined. The words on this page
disappear into night when you close the book.
Black comes from *scorched, burn, a flash* of light before
the darkness takes your hand and strips it to the bone.
If Black had a secret, it would be unknown. A mouth
without a tongue. Your name with no body.

Anita Endrezze

The Secret of Water

I was always afraid of water.
It moves, falling, trickling, dripping,
streaming, pouring, weeping.
Only dead things are still.
Water knows life travels,
goodbye to dust and mud, goodbye
to skin and breath. It becomes
something else: ice, blood,
puddles, tears. Water has depths
beyond us. It's as shallow as love.
It steams between our moist legs,
it finds our names
in nautilus shells, the secret chambers
of our hearts. Water is a sorceress,
transforming salt and minerals
into skins of names, people I know,
me.

Kim Shuck

Dance Poems

I have fasted over these poems fasted and then
Strapped them to my ankles to dance
Can you hear how the words shake they
Shake good and these steps are for a
Purpose that I have chosen I
Shake books shake
Pebble words

We wear our jeans like a calico shirt as if
Our trip to the filling station was a
Treaty negotiation
Stand hipshot pretend to be
Fearless in our various straddled
Decades mantled like
Red shouldered hawks over something we've stooped on

I am the longing pen the
Blue moth of a pen the
Blue panther guiding the water into
Eddies into the river's eye
Swirls with pebble words slip away through
I am the
Prayer and the tobacco remade

We wear our war songs like the
Stars the spirit dog
Scattered up there for all to see even in the
Cities even there and we are not a
Solitary event listening for the best
Rattle poems we wear our
Libraries on our ankles to dance

Kim Shuck

Bridges and Crossroands

WPA bridge over the Neosho I
Stood on it in full flood with my
Dad the water just
Kissing the underside of the boards the
River moans shivering up my legs it stood until a
Flood licked out the
Footings they
Replaced it but when I dream the Neosho the old bridge is there

They took the zinc out until they hit the
Daylight of 3rd street you could
See the crack in the pavement
Looked like another pothole and there was
Sunlight in the mine
Sunlight just there with the
Dull ache of lead and the grim
Scowl of jack

Those cottonmouths know some songs too they
Know some fish songs and once crossing Tar Creek
Bridge a grandma snake got hit by a
Pickup and in her last breaths we
Drove up on her there like a burning
Library her songs falling away in curls
Taken by updrafts like smoke prayers near the water she
Looked me in the heart and whispered just the one secret

Christina Castro
At The Kitchen Table
For Joy Harjo

is where i write. is where i eat my meals alone. this old table has seating for six,
though there's only one of me. it is the first dinette set my grandparents bought
when they moved to L.A., into the Pacoima housing projects. one of the many
benefits of relocation, this now outdated piece of our family history that sits in the
reservation house my grandparents built, but never had a chance to call home.
it's my home now and i love this table with its sturdy chairs, yellow backrests and
the plastic covered seats with pea green flowers. the tabletop with it's blond wannabe
wood finish and slim orange border. some people may think it's ugly but it is precious
to me. i could not imagine writing anywhere else in the house. i think about all the stories
contained in this table and how my own will be added to it's long history. i type them
into the laptop late into the night and write here in a journal when i get up in the
morning.

i trust this table. it holds my secrets.

how many things in this life can we take for certain? how little we know to be true.
people will disappoint us. come and go. waste away before our very eyes.
but not this table. it has always been a part of my life. whether i noticed it or not,
it was here. waiting for me to find it. to honor it with my own gift. i understand now,
this table made it's way back to the rez, just as i have made my way to the rez,
for a reason.

we both know better than to question such things.

we understand the simple gifts, like a good meal or a love poem he'll never read.
we keep each other company on these silent nights,

this table and i.

and the simple acts of reciprocity that sustain us.a

Christina Castro

the night is pink with possibility

off to the west of Jemez,
the sun sets behind the mountain.
in her passing, she leaves a brilliant pink tint to the evening sky.
pink to lavender, to purple, to blue.
i've always hated pink.
but tonight i can't help but embrace its hue.
it makes me want to cry for all the beauty i miss
when i hole myself in my house, and sleep another day away.
it's easier than being awake.
easier than dealing with the feelings inside me.
in the soft, underside of my emotions,
i am pink.
I didn't want to admit it, but it's true.
if you were to peel back my brown skin,
the first thing you'd see is pink.
if i stand in front of the mirror,
open my mouth, and look at my teeth,
they are connected to gums that are pink.
if i reach down between my legs,
and peel back brown lips,
what lies beneath is a bright undeniable pink.
what is it about pink i dislike so much?
is it the whole pink-girl connection?
i never wanted to be a pink kinda girl.
pink is for prissy chicks, with fake nails and frosted lips.
pink is for polo shirts on male queens in brown loafers.
pink is not me.
i am too brown for pink. that's what i like to think.
but as i sit here looking out the window to the west,
at the beauty of this New Mexico night,
i must ask myself,
what i ever had against the little sister of red.
does she remind me of my lost innocence?
my little girl hopes and dreams gone blue?

Devreaux Baker

Counting Moons

Ten moons after
and I am still dreaming
about winter in the mouth
of spring,
still feeling the hooves
of loss stampeding
the bones inside my body
wondering where the dead
journey when they walk
out of the houses of the living
This is the way we learn
how to make sense in a senseless
world, count the moons
that cross the sky and roll
bone dice in the backwater
alleys of our souls until
all our questions of right
and wrong learn lessons
from the shape shifter and
fly out of our doors as birds;
crows or ravens. I am counting
moons until the memory of the
bombing of your sister's village
folds up her tents and finds
a home in someone else's arms.
You wander the hallways
like a lost ghost and ask why
did she want a wedding in a world
made of war? Why did she want
a dress stitched with the dreams
of our people? Why did she work
side by side with all the older

women grinding spices and flattening
dough into bread? Why did she believe
in the possibility of love in the
year of the drone? Mornings I wake
with the smell of cumin and turmeric
marjoram and coriander.
I wake with the call to prayer that signals
forgiveness and a new beginning
for all of us. I walk to the window
of a house in a land that does not
welcome me and whisper the names
of the dead and the living. I fold the
names in my palm and
find you in the kitchen
releasing the smell of spice
into the soul of a world
famished for peace
causing me to feel as hungry
as all the migrant tongues anxious
to be fed words they will be able to
eat as bread and drink as coffee
in this new land.

A Singer's Siren Calling In Marcus Garvey Park; August 24th 2013

for Cecile McLorin Salvant

her voice reminds of a great dancer's supple body
the way it bends itself into syllables, grace notes
extended into flight, phrases spinning high in the moment
when her voice cruised light through space creating melodies, improvising solos so
stunningly elastic, so different, though
her voice echoed familiar clues – bessie, ella, billie, sarah, abby –
threaded through our ears sassy as it eased into lyrics -
wanting someone to be a lollypop she could suck & lick -
then she pulled back to naughty french kisses – oo la la –
sounds of lascivious jelly rolls ala josephine baker,
then, for one so young, she turned on a dime,

became magical, changed again into a bright flower
blooming mysteriously right before our eyes, suddenly
                                            her hypnotic light captured attention,
wouldn't let go when she soared, dipped back down to earth,
became a spiritual song growling deep in the blues dark,
a lover moaning heat, trembling – soaked to the bone with sweat –
before passion leaped into the moment, flipped her tongue risqué,
risky, elongating her vocal sounds into stretching possibilities
steep in a language of outrage, before switching quickly to tender,
love we came to know now in her ancient voice,
an urgent calling, a siren's song igniting cleansing flames,

it was a commanding performance, fierce, compelling,
unafraid, a searing light beckoning to us hours after midnight

Barbara Tran

Unframed

In the Vietnamese language, there is no present
or past tense. Verbs are not conjugated. Time
is discerned through context. Without context,
there is no going or gone or will go; you can only
be. In my family's albums, photos are arranged
in no apparent order. On the left, my family
before a cathedral in Montreal. On the right, my
sisters in saris. Falling out of the album, American
students marching in support of the war in Viet
Nam. About three inches wide with deckle edged
frames, sepia toned photos of people I don't
know but can see in my mother's face. My father
in a cowboy hat in the desert.

JoAnne Balangit

Alice

"So what did you do this weekend?"
I asked her in the hallway so dark her smile
erupted like a puffball. Her padded legs
sprang from the undersized desk. She
expanded like Alice having nibbled
the EAT ME cake. "I saw my Daddy,"
she said and tipped her jellies to show
a bit of sparkle and a bit of tar. "Ah," I nodded.
"So you visit your dad on the weekends?"
"Nope," she replied and the school desk
swallowed her. She twitched like a cornered mouse.

For a time we listened to muddy waves of voices
lap the classroom door. "I seen him from my
bedroom window and I heard his voice." Finally
she spoke. "So I yelled and stuck my hand
outside to wave. But he never turned around.
He went down that sidewalk."

That was twenty years ago and still
I lie in bed some mornings—nice ones
like today, dazzling blue though bitter—
and I search for the face of that man
and the name of that girl, whose name
I did not ask.

Dan Vera

Stain of the Half Life

Examine the oldest petroglyphs:
dim etchings of who we were,
what we killed and gathered.

Immerse yourself in the archives:
vaults of story, art and illumination,
war and peace in form and figure.

Litanate the names of the dead:
the laureled and carelessly forgotten,
the regal and heroic across our ages.

The full scope of our blood's history,
a tenuous smudge on geology,
all this and more we play with

as we power our minutes and days
with materials of deadly decay.
And so make promises for a future

we no more fathom than our past.
We trade expedience with our waste.

The thorium in our reactors
contains a deadly stain
with a half-life of 160,000 years.

Dan Vera

Historical Site #3

Take the third exit off the interstate.
Follow directions to "Pioneer Park."

See the little patch of prairie
preserved to show old wagon ruts.

The women will wear bonnets.
The men will hammer shoes.

They will have the complexion of bleached flour.
Do not ask who's missing.

Note the color of the corn dolls in the gift shop.
Make your way to exits quietly.

Continue on your way.

Dan Vera

Laika

Call me Muttnik.
Call me Hound of the Outer Reaches.

But remind them I was the first
Kudryavka, "Little Curly,"
picked because I survived
the streets of Moscow's cold.

Near starvation, they brought me in
first with food and warmth
than with the celestial promise
of the world's longest walk.

The day before I rose to space
they had me play with children
for the first and last time
squeal and tiny hands for memory.

Then came Cosmodrome,
then cold, then fear, then fire,
then weightlessness and dreams of hunts
beyond the stars.

Tell the story of how I survived
wrapped tight like a gift to the stars
till on the sixth day I expired.

Thomas Johnson

Whitefacedindiansridingfifteenmilestothegal longivingnewmeaningtotwelvehorsepower.

t'ááłá'í _
Pulled from family and healing songs
burned with coals that once warmed the home
cut off like hair, cut out like tongues
unclean, unclean, not pure like
me.

naaki_
the voices lost lie in obedience and despair.
There is no sun, no life in here.
Round faces and coal black eyes
still kept warm today by those blankets,
you know what kind.

táá' _
There on the horizon, new dawn rises,
coated by black feathered crows,
with white faces.

dįį' _
I visit my culture like lions,
caged in a zoo,
itching to come out.
But no one is reaching for the key.
Let them die gracefully,
The lion's roar sounds like a scream.

ashdla_'
Here I am, a man with pen in hand,
wondering why I can't say
"Good morning" without
feeling like a tourist in my own land.
I was not stolen like my uncles and aunts.
But cleverly (subtly) tricked into who I am.
kill the Indian,
save the man.

Linda Weasel Head

Voice Like Rain

for Joy Harjo

Horizon.
Faint was the light.
A narrow knife
slicing my new found university life.
I am circle in a square classroom.
Enemy territory.
A scout for the people.
A hunter. My prey
shape-shifting into books
and numbered footnotes.
Western thought crowds my
Salish roots. *Hold on my girl.*

She walks in bright as eastern sky
like deer guts spilling out life.
An essence, a calm presence.
Her voice like rain
on golden leaves, curling away
from concrete. She speaks mist-like
sweeping dry mesas.
I hear. I eat. I dream
southwest beats
Ortiz. Silko. Momaday
Hold on my girl,
ancestors just
entered the room.
Smoked hides. Sweat grass.
Cedar. Juniper. Sage.
My skin is tearing away.

Read the students
begged one afternoon
Or was it morning in some faraway

dream. She began *New Orleans.*
She became spirit, a long grass dancer
leading the way, right
In front of me. Her voice
touching deep-roots
where I was wrapped
Where I was staked to the ground.

Hostage to gold fever greed.

Ancestors pushed me
Hold on my girl.
You are growing new skin.
Unfold your dormant wings.
Cleansed as her voice
washed over me.
I still hold
We spun children, not gold

Elizabeth Woody

Twanat

Blue Moonlight in swooped clouds thin to dark eagles mating
in crosses of upward elliptical loops.

Beating pulses synchronize heartbeats among the tule reed longhouses.

An old wound in the land healed over years of corruption and charging horse
soldiers. The children ran over the embankment, here.

Alarms were frantic pounding of hooves and rifles. In the spirits silent rising and
cracking bones the valley courses with Nee Mee Poo souls.

At times one hears music in the leaves. It is light tinkles of shell. Rapture.

Run off torrents with moonlight ice. Exhale. Breathe deep, organ pipes moan under
the ribs from church.

The ancestors sing despite conversion.

This is not one voice but the beginning of all voices in unison. Yes, crescendo waves
of spiral utterances of the Plateau canyons. Blue herons rise.

The river returns pervasive with silver and red Nusoox.

Ichiskiin words:
Twanat means to follow, as in ancestral teachings, cultural lifeways
Nee Mee Poo are Nez Perce
Nusoox means salmon

Tanaya Winder

When Angels Speak of Love

I'm pretty sure they didn't mean
drunken hockey fans spraying 57 native children with beer,
taunting, mouthing racial slurs, & phrases like "Go back to the reservation"

If love is all coming and going this is coloniality
starting back at its beginning with children so young they are still learning
the meaning of words like, love and hate. And you gotta hate
the way the world works when some words scar your ears so deeply
that the voice that said them still echoes in your head, still echoes in your head
still echoes in your head.

If love is action and we cannot tell
where one echo ends and begins. Let's think of it like this.
Life begins with a woman giving birth and because of this she is sacred.
Yet, our women are being taken. 1,181 reported missing and murdered
in Canada alone and the numbers here in the US are still unknown.
Underreported not reported but we do have some statistics:
Nearly half of all Native American women have been raped, stalked by
an intimate partner, or beaten.

When angels speak of love I'm certain they didn't mean this.
Our women and children are being traumatized.
1 in 3 Native women will be raped in her lifetime & are 2.5 times more likely
to experience sexual assault crimes compared to all
other races. When does this race to feel safe and survive end?
When you're missing in life and missing in death, where do we begin?

Nowadays when angels try to speak of love my ears strain to hear
anything over the national news and media that barely, if ever mention us
and I wonder if the silence is how we eventually disappear.

Before angels speak of love and us, they press their lips to the solar system
then shout courage is a circle we must keep coming back to, a circle we keep
coming back to, we keep coming back to, we keep the memory of the missing
stitched to the top of our chests pulsing with each breath we take
praying that hers is a path that ends in a union and reunion, in coming back home.

Tanaya Winder

The Milky Way Escapes My Mouth

whenever two lips begin to form your name
I cough stars lodged deep within my lungs. They rush
        from tongue weighted in dust, words
                I didn't ask

where are you going? or notice the blank spaces
in your breathing as you slept. They say
        the more massive the star, the shorter
                the lifespan.

They have greater pressure on their cores. Yours burned
so brightly I should have known you'd collapse, disappear
        into image, a black hole dissolving
                trace amounts.

I am left stargazing five times a day for years. Catalogue
phrases. Chart each word. Label every facial expression.
        Telescope until eyes bleed constellations
                even then

I can't navigate my way into understanding light years –
how we let darkness slip in. Is it madness to wonder
        if it ever really happened? You, a shadow never leaving
                until I

inserted continents between us. *I lost you* in the crevice
between night and day. You died while I was sleeping
        dreaming of a galaxy far far away where
                love eclipses.

A rising tide of longing fills my body, bones, the ribs
sheltering the cave within me echoing. Each night,
        I open mouth sky-wide to swallow stars
                and sing

to the moon a story about the light of two people
who continue to cross and uncross in their falling
        no matter how unstable
                in orbit.

LeAnne Howe

Upon Leaving The Choctaw Homelands, 1831, The Major Speaks

AFTER DEPARTURE, TICKET IS NON REFUNDABLE
NO SHOW MEANS NO REFUND, FORFEITURE
PENALTIES AND CANCELATIONS APPLY AT WILL
CHANGES SUBJECT TO FINES AND
DEATH

Nakfi, Brother, As He Helps Sister Load The Cart

Our leaving will be sung in every church pew like a hymn.

Intek, Sister, As She Helps Brother Pack

Our leaving will be sung by every President, every Supreme Court Justice, every hangaround -
the-fort lawyer, every cavalry officer, every merchant, every Wall Street nymph,
every thief among thieves, every hazardous waste CEO, every medical waste CEO, every
stockholder of the new wasted lands, every rat that shimmied off the ships from Spain,
France, Alsace, Norway, Denmark, Sweden, every pox that crawled off English blankets
and onto our hands.
Our homelands will sing a heart song of sorrow,
And sing,
And sing,
And sing,
She is singing still.

Ishki, Mother, Looks Homeward

They moved into our log cabin yesterday. Yelping like young puppies at play, they tore
down the center pole of our Chief's dance ground, the one with the gar carved atop.
Burned it for firewood. Joyous barking. But we could hear the gar roiling in the flames,
close to the surface as if he were still in Atchafalaya. Gar, he moves slowly except when
striking at prey. Now he soars high on a draft of air carried on wings of cedar ash.
Heading west.

Intek, Sister, Fingers Her White Apron

Brother, before you strap the burden basket to *Naholla?** cart, who will we become now
that we are leaving *Yakni Achukma?**

*Naholla is stingy in Choctaw. It's a word used to reference "white people."
**Yakni Achukma is good land in Choctaw.

Chukchu Imoshi, Maple Tree Uncle, Helps Brother and Sister

Some may call us a people who left our mother, our homelands, for a linen promise.
But I
like it that if we leave, the habits of our diligence on the land will remain private.
Anonymous. Hidden to foreigners. *Hatak okla hut okchaya bilia hoh-illi bila. We are ever living,
ever dying, ever alive.*

Yummak osh alhpesa, that is it

Intek, Sister, Runs To Catch Up
But how long wills the connection between land and people, in which direction will we
look to imagine our past. Our future?

Ishke, Mother, One Step Ahead

See Hiloha, Thunder,
See Malatha, Lightning,
We will be as they,
Our season will return
And return,
And return,
Is returning still.

Yummak osh alhpesa, that is it

River Allen

The Last Flight of Cranes

Dedicated to Ozaawaajijaak of the White Crane Clan

He's singing about the Cambodian Jungle again,
the Chippewa man roosting on the porch of the rehab center
packed with war veterans, strapped to their wheelchairs,
basking their boney cages under the knotted eye of the sun.
"The leeches on our legs would swell this big."
The old soldier spread his hands wide, three inches, then six.

> *One warm breath*
> *if held long enough,*
> *can keep a man floating*
> *on the rim of the world*
> *for seventy-two years.*

Hollow cheeks, labored smile,
avian legs, harvested above the knee by diabetes,
sits a silver-haired bird trapped in a clotted
nest of quills and scarred flesh,
wearing his Purple Heart, losing his way
on the same path of forgotten words.

> *"It's my turn to walk point, Simon,"*
> he says to the empty space next to him.
> *"This time I won't let you down."*

Simon died in '66 on a ridge north of Saigon.
After two failed marriages and five children,
Simon becomes the only name the old Chippewa remembers.
And back in the day, after enough whiskey, he'd forget that too.

Strange and secret his words sometimes sound, twisting in the wind.

> *"When the circle of life is complete,"* the elders would say,
> *"You will start walking backwards, talking backwards.*
> *And you will know it is time to return home."*

One day the old bird took flight,
withered brown fingers reaching skyward, sweat
stench of so much exertion after all these years
trying to get his too small wings to carry him away.

> *"In the end, every wrong turn will be the right one,"*
> he whispers with his crazy, morphine eyes.

An angel in the form of a crane, gliding over the water,
he rose with the mist, dingy white feathers
barbed over the surface through
earths' layers of human tears and laughter,
freed from his drugged haze.

Folding arcs soar higher...
                    higher...
he joins the others in a broken line of cranes,
dreaming their way back home.

Rebeccca Seiferle

Military Formation on Gediminas Street

It was foolish, for I'd seen the men in military
formation taking up the sidewalk, marching
toward us, while another man with a mega horn,
like a parrot transported to his hand, capered
in the gutter, giving them orders, but as if he,
monkey enthusiasm and all, were just the puppet,
barking out the orders the cadre
of the silently marching willed him to say,
but I went to the ATM anyway, needing money
for the morning taxi to begin our journey
home. My son and I had been so happy,
all that warm afternoon strolling through
the amber shops, bits of fossilized tree resin
in our bags, bits of the ancient sea goddess
for everyone we loved at home, and I didn't
want to be thrown off my own path by this brigade
of men--dressed as what? Military men
in street clothes? It was a day of mimicry,
of dressing up, of bachelor parties hunting
like those we'd encountered earlier, where
young men played at knights in shining armor
to get young women to sign their garters.
But there was no camouflage in these joyless
skinheads, neo-Nazi-want-to-be's
who periodically yelled *Jude Raus* in in this "Jerusalem
of the North," so few Jews, so few left, since1943.
I thought I could outrace them, but the ATM's
capitalist logic could not be hurried, though my son
hissed, *hurry, hurry*, when suddenly a siren
wailed in my ear. Weirdly I thought
perhaps a police car had driven up to disperse
the group militarizing the sidewalk
as I grasped the money in my hand, but
the man with the mega horn was blasting
the back of my head. My son turned to him

and said *excuse me,* and for a moment I feared
furious civility would be met by mayhem,
but the man stepped back, as if startled by English,
as if he'd thought he was harassing only his own people,
whoever he thought that was. The group went on,
"we were small potatoes," the man now trying
to make a joke of it, as we escaped to our apartment.
My head was still ringing and ringing from the mega horn,
but when my son said *don't let it ruin everything,*
I heard him, fighting for the sweetness of our days together,
here, in this city, this country, a month of walking
in amber light or having our dinner among the wasps
that swarmed the café but did not sting, love's quiet
insistence to not let hatred ruin anything.

Rebeccca Seiferle

1118 Days, A Handful of Blossoms Tossed Over My Head

1.

I must have been running a fever last night
in the consequence of days
spent sweating until my clothes soured while I weeded

the yard and cleaned the house for a landlady who would keep
the deposit anyway. Turning into a merely
functional body,

laboring until its right foot swelled as its lower
vertebrae locked up, the knee giving out, with a kind
of hitch on the stair. . .

How it went on, no relief
from the heat, one work replaced by another kind
of counting pennies, the anxiety about

the this and the that, even to where the cups should go
in the overcrowded new cupboard. When I moved in with you,
I expected to be only happy, to flower into

our hours, not the cramp and sting of work
work to make the 'marriage' work, narrowing
to the persistent complaint, the rolling of your eyes

back into the sigh of the sink.

2.

What I'm saying is this morning, just now
I'm sick of the cold, I want to flower and flower,
the way the clouds

at the base of the mountains seem to emerge like the breath
of the earth itself, though each cloud is as heavy
as a pod of blue whales.

In the ocean
of being that hovers over our heads, the weight of what is

impending and falling rests on the shoulders
of those waiting at bus stops
to begin their workday. How it hovers, the weight of
necessity, as if it were the shadow of the shadow

of a feather falling from the wing of a hummingbird
driven from meadow to meadow to find the thousands of flowers,
it has to sip in the course of an hour just to stay alive.

Walking from bus stops, the laborers of morning
and night break stones on the city streets, the laborers
of afternoon and evening tend to the bodies of others. None of them

are paid a living wage, waxing the unwanted
hair from a woman's chin or unraveling the predictable
knot in a man's neck, or bringing the soup purged

of bell peppers, chili floating like a red skin on its pure
consommé, these servants of the body, their own
and others, like the dollar bills being slipped into g-strings

snug against the hip, small change in the bones, and a five-dollar
bill stuffed between the breasts.

3.

The sky island floats
in its ring of clouds, and in the rain, for a moment,
the desert is relieved of its fevers,

and I think it has never happened
that the gaze of the western world has fallen upon the body
with the tenderness of this rain falling. . .

Even the gentlest of saints at the end of his life
will say that his only regret is not having been kinder
to 'brother ass' and by 'brother ass,' means his own body,

as if it were the animal he rode in on.
It's all the thinking the body endures: how we think of
the body like a pinched nerve

or an empty pocket that nickels and dimes. Another shift,
and $18 in tips doesn't make up for your bills that are due, or those hours
for which you're paid nothing.

4.

Neck, it's always the shoulders and neck,
you sit at the table holding your wrists against the side of a glass
full of ice water, while your arms and elbows ache.

In your hands, I unravel; you feel the knot at each point
along my scapula and each hurt flares up,
each arguing moment

has left the scald of your tongue, the tip of your finger
to char the shadow of a shadow on the wall
of my back. Oh let, your hands take back

what they have given, unweaving the snarled
loom of my muscles…

and let me make my hand a hummingbird
to brush the flower of your face.

Marilyn Nelson

Violin

"*Violin*," giclee print, Scott Kahn, 2013

Like susurrating brushes on a drum,
the rustling autumn leaves translate a breeze
from the silent sign-language of the clouds.
Aching under January snow,
wind-moved trunks groan like old men getting up.
Staccato February branches click.
April comes in on pitter-pattering feet.
Late summer storms thunder raucous applause.

From the first spring tingle of rising sap
through flowering passion to fruit cradled seed,
season to season, year to year cycling,
the maple and spruce trees on the far shore
rehearse earth's unchanging continuo.
Tough luck, for the wood of a violin,
doomed forever to perform human music.

Patricia Spears Jones

Blossom In The Gyre

Speak of cataclysms and Catastrophes
Blasted bodies and hearts made of platinum—perfect
For earrings, cufflinks, consciousness of senators
Who speak of person hood and democracy
As pregnant women are imprisoned and voters'
Names removed from the record.

What are they to make of poets slinging
Words commanding moist earth for walking
A forest to house a country of animals
A place for the wounding and wounded

Oh wary keening brightens voices
Lips and tongues as portals
To blossoms in the heart
Butterflies in the lungs
Hearts pulsate Hearts pulsate
One and one and one and one &
Daily the petals open
Daily the butterflies travel

Across a world that too often
Beats the earth with heavy vehicles
Scorches forests to rid ancient trees
Of enemies. Waste uncultivated food
That would nurture many.

And yet these sisters singing
As if songs were pulled from
The deepest well of memory
Of butterflies, blossoms, the splendor
Of horses—the year of the horse
Sends them across deserts and mountains
Into the city's heart and out where
The houses stand resolute, apart.

And their singing becomes prayer
For many who need a place for the divine
And their singing becomes a loom
For many who need to a coat of many colors
And their singing loud in outburst
For those who demand justice.
And their singing creates the possibility
Of a vision of peace.
And their song sung over and over
Speaks loudly terrible knowledge of war.

Early in this new millennium, the terrible
Knowledge of war is crafted into
Coffins for butterflies, blossoms.

Divination in the keening
Sisters with horse knowledge
Land knowledge
Knowledge of the Creator's plan
Sisters open your portals
Blossom as you have done
In so many dominions
Let the butterflies find their ways.

Francisco X. Alarcón

Impure Poetry

full
of nails
locks

thimbles
mosaics
clocks

maps
compasses
holes

smiles
teardrops
face slapping

poetry
bound
to things

dreams
misfortunes
lives

of men
women
and kids

alive
dead
to be born

Poesía Impura

llena
de clavos
cerrojos

dedales
azulejos
relojes

mapas
compases
agujeros

sonrisas
lágrimas
bofetadas

poesía
vinculada
a las cosas

los sueños
las desgracias
las vidas

de hombres
mujeres
y niños

vivos
muertos
por nacer

T.R. Hummer

Fisher Cat

Dead center in my insomnia her interior scream
    crowns in her throat, and the bedroom dissolves.
As deep in woods as the amygdala in the brain, the fisher cat
    is God's pure sentience of terror. Through her
God is instructed in *freeze* and *leap* and *claw*, for every atom
    of creation is bonded with fear. Not cat but weasel, she
Is the avatar of adrenalin and cortisol. Even in her lair, asleep,
    her head is toward the portal and her dreaming eyes are open.
For holy horror of you, Lord, she will rip your face from your skull.
    Live in her. You will learn *quiver, crouch*, and *leap*,
You will vibrate with her voice, which is a refuge and a weapon.
    This is why you made her. Go to her. I will pray for you, Lord.
Even from the core of her nightmare, she is eternally aware of you.

T.R. Hummer

Scene

The woman liked to make love late, after everyone
    was asleep, including the man, whom she would wake
By throwing one leg across him, whispering their private language
    which is the code of all lovers, until he returned
From the other world, where his ghosts clung to him.
    she was stronger than all the magnificent dead, and ripped him
Out of his own future, though the spirits moaned
    in exactly the same key she moaned in, being entered.

Annie Finch

Amulet For Brave Women

Women have voices it's time to believe in.
Wise women's strong words, spoken out clear and
steady,
move us with generous ways of achieving.
Women have voices it's time to believe in,
braiding sweet worlds. This brave, loving weaving
is singing our lives back, and women are ready—
women have voices. It's time to believe in
wise women's strong words, spoken out clear and
steady.

Doug Anderson

Northern Lights

I'd just move up from New York
where in eight years
I'd scarcely seen the sky,
maybe one dirty star
framed between two buildings,
but nothing like this,
with the sky cleared
by cold to perfect black.
Ice on the lake
was moaning in its labor
as it cracked and shifted
and I thought
maybe it was praising
what the three of us
looked up to see.
One whispered
"It's caused by solar storms"
as if science would somehow
damp the awe and save us
from enchantment..
I might as well have been
the Inuit who before
we half killed him
with our culture
might have been out
in his kayak and looked up.
The sea silent and only felt
beneath him, rocking mother.
If I'd known the words,
I'd have sung some ancient thing
and named it. Okay, I'll try:
hard to escape the signs
we've come to know it by,
say, "curtains." No,
and I say, No, such things

agreed upon too long
kill it. There is a place
in us where feeling
becomes language,
where words are hauled
out of their ovens
and the ash cleaned off,
where flesh becomes sound,
that point, where Blake said,
*"My heart knock'd against
the root of my tongue" --
that place. What I saw:
magenta, yes, violet,
and stars above which
green washed over
like clear surf
above luminescence.
A robe dropping to the floor
to reveal more than
I ever wanted. Aurora
yes, who invites prayer.
Like that place
when you are first in love
and don't know
what's happening to you.
There, and where God
does not hate the body
but welcomes it back
into all it means
to be a cogitating animal
in this short life. That.
I give up. I can't speak
but only be, and be silent.*

Alfred Corn

Beadwork Song

a cento drawn from Native American poems

The mountain trembled and shook with pain.
I and my name whistle along the road of stars.

*

Beside me, the mountain stream,
the feathery mountain stream.

*

The salmon came to look for a dancer.
Life, my one and only tree! Around you we dance.

*

Child, sit down in the mouth of the sky!
The hawks turn their heads to look back on their flight

*

Look at me closely, my friends; examine me,
and let's understand that we are bound in this together.

*

Our song will enter that distant land
and roll the lake in waves.
Fire-fly, fire-fly, light me on my way

Marilyn Kallet

How To Get Heat Without Fire

Beneath the dark floor
there has always been love,
but the trick is
how to get down to it?
Shall I tear my way down
like a tiger clawing
the floorboards, when this
tearing down is what scarred you?
Whose mother is there
in the dark trying hard
to hide you from the memory
of the floorboards in flame?
How to get heat without fire?
To coax light open?
To ease you new into
the world if I am not
a mother, or a beloved?
Pull back? Peel back dead
bark, pull back the boards
we trample, throw each other
down on and through some days?
Turn the floor into a pool
we can dive deep into,
cradle the mothers,
let the animals swim their ways?
Has music ever saved anyone?
Then I will reenter my life
as sound,
as notes strung like pearls
that you have yearned
to enter.
I will be sound,
I will be sound,
and silence,
listening.

from HOW TO GET HEAT WITHOUT FIRE, New Millenium Women Poets Series,
1996

Marilyn Kallet
Unusual

1.

Cold white sun. Pam's off at the sperm bank
checking "Anglo-Saxon."
A wary shopper, she passed on the box marked

"unusual."

How sick I am of categories!
Do the trees care that the sky has no roots?
Pines and sky interplay, windy winter blues.
Why not say "breath" for sky and branches?

Why call me "slow" when I may be racing toward

another life?

Oh, I can see myself in your rear-view mirror,
plucky like a sperm on my way to the bank,
determined, it's pay day,
breathe, breathe, wiggle wiggle, I'm an unusual

metaphor,

Reeboks instead of flagella.

Pam calls back—she's learned that "unusual"
means Native American.
It's 1941, Berlin, and I'm
unusual, hell, we're all a heartbeat away
from unusual. We all love our children past
categories, we'd invent any subterfuge to save them,
give them our breath, swallow this white sun,
dragons breathing fire on the Klan, a belch
for that boy
in Heather's class who said the Jews were stupid,
better save a candleflame for Mrs. English
so she'll recant the narrow outline,
reteach the whole Fourth Grade—

this time that writing outside

the margin

is lovely, the practice of wind and trees and sun,
unusual grandmothers and grandfathers
praying for the shining mothers and fathers
on our way to God-knows-where.

2.

In bed, when I tell him about my sperm-walk,
my concern about suddenly seizing the *macho*—
do I secretly want to be a man?
Lou says, "There's a big difference between
being a sperm and being a man."
"What's the difference?"
"A man is alive, a sperm, debatable."
"And sperm don't know where they're going,"
I add." "Neither do most men,"
says Lou.

from HOW TO GET HEAT WITHOUT FIRE, New Millenium Women Poets Series,
1996

William Pitt Root

Crossing The Rez

For Joy Harjo

I was hitching a ride toward twilight
southeast of Billings, middle of November,
when a pickup let me toss my gear in back.
I climbed up into the cab boozy with two old boys,
Country Western FM blaring sad songs of love.
The driver's sidekick cackled "Cold enough out there
to chrome a bobcat's balls." He hoisted a pint of
high noon moonshine, shoved it into my chapped hands.
It purely thawed my tongue as they both jawboned
down the road, pointing out into the uniform blue dark
toward Custer's Last Stand. "Never trust no Injun,
bud, don't matter *how* cold it gits," they soberly
advised, shaking their heads and slowing down,
dropping me off there, smack on the Rez, at sunset.

And there I stood the best part of a bad hour
until along came the first car that stopped,
a rumpled one-eyed station wagon, front bumper
dangling, muffler skidding ice-glazed blacktop
just like a kid's sparkler in the dark.
                              "Hop in, par'ner,"
and in I hopped, stiff with cold, duffle on my lap,
all the wide dark faces, in front and back,
flat and friendly as old Hank Williams
carried on about good love gone bad again
from a scratchy speaker loose on the dash.
One popped the top on a Bud for me as gradually
we picked up speed, tranny wailing like a wolf,
everybody howling themselves into Hank's fix,
off-key and flat, while we hurtled through
the dark in a one-eyed comet.
                              "Where you headed?"

"Sheridan." He nodded, smiled.
"Thing is, par'ner, we can't take you there.
Off-rez cops, they catch us in this heap,
hey, it's bail-time in the Rockies. When
we drop you at Wyola, just
remember this: Cold as your ass gits
              don't park it in no cowboy pickup,
you'll do just fine. And do say Howdy
for us 'In'dins' to all the pretty girls
you meet on down the line."

Lodge Grass, Crow Nation

from STRANGE ANGELS, Wings Press, 2014

Clarence Major

Swans

In your dream background music of singing swans!
The ancients sacrificing animals then each other!
You were visiting that old foster nurse, Nature!
For sure golden slumber kissing your eyes!
Coleridge's swans singing to you as they die?
But are you a wandering sacrificial minstrel?
And was Keats' whispering to you with his "O soft embalmer!"
Surely, you were sinking into a deeper sleep!
Then waking suddenly set you free.

Carmen Calatayud
Fire Flood

I dream of a flood, you
rolled in a powder blue blanket
on the black vinyl couch,
parked in front of a TV
that shows where poker cards
flicker and fly while you
drink your third bottle of beer.

Monsoon water washes away
the screen that soothes your system.
In the empty space
where the TV lived,
I dance by lamp light,
leap onto the coffee table
to pirouette into still dry air.
Pink bruises decorate my spine.
My back was in pieces last year,
put together like a stained-glass puzzle
and now moves like perfunctory
chunks of a plodding drive shaft.

I pause at my altar for the bones
of women I'll never meet. You say
you don't remember how you lit
their skin on fire, apologized
after second-degree burns
turned the smooth skin of their legs
red as wild sockeye salmon flesh.

I try to forget that you almost
turned me into a ripe hibiscus flame.
I don't know what your silence means
any more than I know how the grey
clouds of salt blinding my eyes
might eventually storm to release.

Bryce Milligan

Trying Not To Fall

for Joy Harjo

There is a woman with a saxophone
blowing the blues out of time
raising tones like thunderheads
and tones like lightning,
tones like the gray mist
rising on an Oklahoma river.

There is a woman with a saxophone,
golden horn handed down
one prophet to another
one shaman to the next
beginning as a scrannel flute
golden reed from the Chattahoochee
drawn at dawn and cured inside
a medicine bundle somewhere
in America, somewhere
in time
flint carved its first song,
the song of awakening
after long sleep, after death.

There is a woman with a saxophone
breathing in the same air
drawn through the sacred stem
when no white hand had laid claim
or shed blood anywhere
in America.

There is a woman with a saxophone,
woman of wind and water
blowing the blues out of time
woman with hair like the raven

that hangs in the sky calling the future
as he sees it, hair blue
blue as blackbird wings in sunshine
with eyes like black holes
in time, ends and beginnings
quick as grace notes.

There is a woman with a saxophone
on the banks of the Muscogee
rising into the cloud of her music
rising like sacred smoke
rising like stomp dance bonfire flames
rising like warriors bound
for the long paths of the milky way.
There is a woman with a saxophone
trying
not to fall.

Bill Wetzel

Ghost Flats

a variation on Themes by James Welch

they shook the green tree down.
its spindly bole forked back golden
in crystal's lunar waves.
the dirt is dead, further out wind
is all the rage, lethal in the dust.

we raced a century, skinning together stories
the vital wages of seared sin, no one civic
spoke of our good side, winter jingled
meaning into the wind. scattered bones
leave no sign, famous in my blood
mapped like smoke from narrow wind.

men wept like public saints, women like lucky
numbers in electric flame, jumping against
the new-found luck of sky and mortgaged gold.
he swung philosophic, implied in exile chrome
wind decorating stunted light, dreaming
winter against a world of silent legends.

those songs busy with knives, stars that
fell cheap when eyes color a winter blue.
starved visions, meaningless tapping
in recollections of myths, so simple
beneath his bleached broken shack.

No room for a wandering race dying
from imitated life. images clattered,
muscling winter red blood like rain
in my bones. I'll move on. the renegade
astounded as real words create winehappy
life, where battered dreams must end.

Joy Harjo Poetry Prize: 1st Place

Terri Kirby Erickson

After The Explosion

for Tommy, 1959 – 1980

My brother, splayed on the concrete like a bearskin
rug, body broken, eyes filmy, died in a river of red
that flowed as if the summer air were a vampire,
crazed with hunger. It ran in rivulets down the driveway,
into a street lined with neighbors upon whose
retinas the image of his death was burned. Perhaps
his spirit lingered for a while, leery of its new and
borderless dimensions—entered a tool lying on the
garage floor, marveling at the chill of his cold, metal
skin. Next, the bee flying over the heads of paramedics
frantically working, the buzz like nothing he ever felt,
a rumbling deep in his chest, the clap of wings much
softer than hands. And after that, a few more stops—
the cement statue of the shy girl our mother bought
for the garden, the dog next door that wouldn't stop
barking, the taste of its pink tongue strange and wild
in a mouth that opened wider than any door. And out
of that dog's mouth my brother shot into the sky like
a bottle rocket, though none of us looked up. How I
wish we could have seen his swift ascent, the pressures
of his life: go to school, get a job, conform, conform,
conform—lift like a piano from his chest, his soul
rising weightless, without impediment, until he reached
the stars from which we all are made and zoomed by
them, faster than any plane he dreamed as a boy, to fly.

Joy Harjo Poetry Prize: 2nd Place

Chen Chen

First Light

I like to say we left at first light
    with Chairman Mao himself chasing us in a police car,
my father fighting him off with firecrackers,
    even though Mao was already over a decade
dead, & my mother says all my father did
    during the Cultural Revolution was teach math,
which he was not qualified to teach, & swim & sunbathe
    around Piano Island, a place I never read about
in my American textbooks, a place everybody in the family
    says they took me to, & that I loved.
What is it, to remember nothing, of what one loved?
    To have forgotten the faces one first kissed?
They ask if I remember them, the aunts, the uncles,
    & I say *Yes it's coming back*, I say *Of course*,
when it's *No not at all*, because when I last saw them
    I was three, & the China of my first three years
is largely make-believe, my vast invented country,
    my dream before I knew the word *dream*,
my father's martial arts films plus a teaspoon-taste
    of history. I like to say we left at first light,
we had to, my parents had been unmasked as the famous
    kung-fu crime-fighting couple of the Southern provinces,
& the Hong Kong mafia was after us. I like to say
    we were helped by a handsome mysterious Northerner,
who turned out himself to be a kung-fu master.
    I don't like to say, I don't remember *crying*.
No embracing in the airport, sobbing. I don't remember
    feeling bad, leaving China.
I like to say we left at first light, we snuck off
    on some secret adventure, while the others were
still sleeping, still blanketed, warm
    in their memories of us.

What do I remember of crying? When my mother slapped me
     for being *dirty, diseased, led astray by Western devils,*
a dirty, bad son, I cried, thirteen, already too old,
     too male for crying. When my father said *Get out,*
never come back, I cried & ran, threw myself into night.
     Then returned, at first light, I don't remember exactly
why, or what exactly came next. One memory claims
     my mother rushed into the pink dawn bright
to see what had happened, reaching toward me with her hands,
     & I wanted to say *No. Don't touch me.*
Another memory insists the front door had simply been left
     unlocked, & I slipped right through, found my room,
my bed, which felt somehow smaller, & fell asleep, for hours,
     before my mother (anybody) seemed to notice.
I'm not certain which is the correct version, but what stays with me
     is the leaving, the cry, the country splintering.
It's been another five years since my mother has seen her sisters,
     her own mother, who recently had a stroke, who has trouble
recalling who, why. *I feel awful,* my mother says,
     not going back at once to see her. But too much is happening here.
Here, she says, as though it's the most difficult,
     least forgivable English word.
What would my mother say, if she were writing a poem? This poem?
     How would her voice sound? Which is really to ask, what is
my best guess, my invented, translated (Chinese-to-English,
     English-to-English) mother's voice? She might say:
We left at first light, we had to, the flight was early,
     in early spring. Go, my mother urged, *what are you doing,*
waving at me, crying? Get on that plane before it leaves without you.
     It was spring & I could smell it, despite the sterile glass
& metal of the airport—scent of my mother's just-washed hair,
     of the just-born flowers of fields we passed on the car ride over,
how I did not know those flowers were already
     memory, how I thought I could smell them, boarding the plane,
the strange tunnel full of their aroma, their names
     I once knew, & my mother's long black hair—so impossible now.
Why did I never consider how different spring could smell, feel,
     elsewhere? First light, last scent, lost
country. First & deepest severance that should have
     prepared me for all others.

Hope Maxwell Snyder

Blue Nights

Neruda's color was blue, sky blue, dark blue like the color of the night,
blue like the sweater rolled under his feet, blue like a hurt dog, blue
like a silent blue shore, and blue like the ocean, sometimes sinister and endless
sometimes crystalline, turquoise, the sand on the bottom clean as a blank sheet.
Like the poet, the ocean always changes. Even his name,
taken from Jan Neruda who lived and wrote in Prague
where there is a street named after him, though when tourists see it
they think of Pablo, who, at the age of twenty, wrote:
"Tonight, I can write the saddest lines. Write, for instance:
the night is starred, and blue stars tremble in the distance."
At nine, I knew this poem by heart and stood in the living room in Bogotá
reciting it for my grandfather who loved to hear it after work.
We lived with him, and he taught me to repeat, remember,
enunciate, where to pause, what syllables to stress. Evenings
before dinner, I recited the poem without paying attention to the words,
except what followed what, never wondering if my grandfather shared
Neruda's longing, never thinking of a woman who lived somewhere else
in the city and looked too worn out for love, nor the woman
who shared my grandfather's bed and looked too fat for love.
But he gave me Neruda's music, and Neruda gave me blue nights,
blue _____, blue _____,
and the words to describe your body, how it tastes of wine and apples.

Linda Hogan and Joy Harjo Interview

Conducted by email January 2015

Linda--I am ready to begin a conversation for Cutthroat and it would be a very welcome diversion at this point. Thank you for everything. I returned and became sick the next day and am in bed most all-day still. I think my body is grieving.

I wonder why is the underlying impulse of your work and what does you inner self tell you to write? I am especially considering your memoir and the way it moves and how you came into the world on the strains of music. Do you consider what it is your work is driven by?

Joy--*We've probably had an ongoing conversation for years as we have continued writing since our first meeting. We have a similar sense of purpose. And grief is at the root of so much that we write, not necessarily by choice but by the nature of being indigenous to these lands. Our tribal communities are absolutely tied into the ecosystems within which we lived. We took (and take) care of those forces and they in turn us. When we were forcibly removed, as our peoples were, those lands and we suffered, together. It has to be put right. One of my favorite books is <u>Karma and Reincarnation</u> by a Shinto Buddhist priest, Hiroshi Motoyama who speaks about this directly, how there is national, racial, and geographic karma. Karma really translates to me as "story". And stories will happen or want to be born to even things out, or, for balance.*

Linda--That is a very heavy way to begin a conversation. Perhaps our souls have been talking without our presence. Karma is a very good story if you have it as a belief system. I would like to never be fixed in my beliefs and to be fluid, although I did love the Shinto shrines and the monks in Japan when I was there. And I do love the Dalai Lama for having such a life that has allowed for great pain and great humor and always compassion.

I think compassion is the story and that it is also in our lands. When I think of the richness of that earth we had to leave, the great forests, the great waters, I still feel that loss. I write it. But when I think of settlers moving into our homes while we still lived there, I go into a state of great shock at their willingness to take and take. And then in Oklahoma, I don't know the Creek experience, only our region. But we had constant war with plains Indians whose land it was. And then when the Dawes Acts was passed, another great land theft, my family had to constantly watch the lands because of sooners and squatters who tried to settle illegally. But in between that was the civil war. So, that is history. And maybe it is the root of our very being, so maybe it is what we write.

I want to write the compassion part and not only grief, or at least to transform grief into something beautiful, because I am in love with everything on the earth and nothing has taken that away from me. I do my chores, take care of horses, people, and have even participated with the ants in their underground building outside, passing small sticks to the ones at the hole like the other ants. Then I studied them in books. From the thirties on. Different material the EO Wilson. But interesting to me. And then I nursed an elk after a wolf attack out by the horse shed. That is after they killed a deer earlier and while I was typing. I write about all this, too.

I see that your reach is so far in your writing, up to the skies, across the land like a wonderful traveler, and you are. Your work is like your music, improvisational. I remember when we thought about the traditional music in our poetry, back years ago. And now we've each created our own, mine more inner, perhaps, and yours like the instruments and with all that amazing sound.

But then, as I think of it, don't you think we should write more love poems????

Joy—*Always more love poems!!*

Okay. These questions regarding my work and writing habits are more innately answerable, than how to address the grief of the earth, of indigenous peoples, and the whole damned colonized world. This grief cannot be contained in words though words are containers that often bear immense weight. The sharpest grief can be the relatively small, made of the detritus of human interaction. Massacres start small and internal.

Writing, for me, in whatever form: memoir, poem, or song, emerges from a similar impulse. I believe my root impulse is to bring beauty into the world, or rather to recognize it, because it is here. I believe beauty is the final truth.

I came to writing through music. I love dancing and rhythm as much as anything else. I can be most free when dancing, and as I developed saxophone, my voice, and writing I have begun to feel a similar freedom in those arts. It's a freedom without judgment--I am just with the music that is contained in words and groups of words, sound, and meaning.

I've often argued with my inner self. Who is my inner self anyway? It is so complex yet it is a coherent spirit. It is wiser than me and is a wise ass too. It's well traveled through knowledge of many realms of time and space. It is creative and it is compassionate. It does not argue. No need. It just is and when I go there---there we are--

For a while I was thrown in with lots of hip hop spoken word events. I am a strange bird there. I appear from a different age, from writing acid rock songs for an Indian school band to which the painter Dan Namingha belonged. I'm considered a performer, not necessarily a performance poet. (Maybe I am....) I'm older. Their beats dance different--we're all dancing—

I've always been different no matter where I get put. I'm a musician but I play saxophone and I'm a "girl". Where's my guitar? I am a native musician but I don't look like a Plains male warrior! And, I'm a "girl". I am an American poet, but I am indigenous. And...a "girl". And then there's age---

The inner self says all of that is bullshit. Fashion comes and goes. A good song is a good song. A good poem is a good poem. A good story will find its way through the maze of human meaning.

The original inspiration for my poetry was music. My mother wrote songs. If I think about her process I saw her at the kitchen table at her typewriter. However, most of her songs were written in ballpoint pen ink on the back of envelopes and those cheap lined stationary pads for small letter envelopes. The typewriter was for official business. She sent of inquiries to companies in Hollywood. Maybe she typed the final drafts of lyrics.

She did not play an instrument. She sang melodies. One of the top Broadway musical writers I know writes his songs this way. He has no formal knowledge of music.

I find that my knowledge of my lack of knowledge gets in the way.

I came to poetry first through songwriting. At Indian school, or the old IAIA I did not take creative writing. I was a 2-D major, then wound up in the first native drama and dance troupe. I attempted some songwriting for an all IAIA band. They were acid rock songs. Belinda Gonzales and I were the unofficial go-go dancers for the band.

Do I write everyday? No. But I try to keep a continuum. The flow is better when I write daily as writing is a communication device between the spiritual world and me. Of course all of this is the spiritual world: the good, the bad, the ugly, and the terrifyingly beau-

*tiful parts of it. I have no typical day. When I'm home I prefer to have the morning to
write, think, read, listen, and then the afternoon to work on music. These days I seem
to get buried in obligations and administrative efforts. And then there is teaching, which
involves traveling, and then traveling to perform. Travel is much more difficult than it
was five or ten years ago. There's all the security layers and the airlines are much more
unreliable. I am inspired by travel. My new mantra is "Everything is my art." I say this
to myself when I feel torn by obligations.*

*Transformative process is also an impulse of my writing, with everything I've written,
culminating in my memoir <u>Crazy Brave</u>. I sense that after that memoir there is a huge
shift in my writing. One of my close readers commented that when she read my forthcom-
ing book of poetry, <u>Conflict Resolution for Holy Beings</u> she heard my heart. She said it
was the first collection of mine she's read that sounded like me, with no guardedness. Our
writing can transform others, but it also transforms the writer.*

*Linda, in your latest book of poetry, <u>Dark, Sweet, New and Collected Poems</u> the first
line of the first poem opening the new poems section is "If you think I am going to write
about someone's god….", plants me absolutely in Oklahoma.*

Were these poems written from Oklahoma?

*I know that you returned home, before I did. And you have returned to Colorado after
being tested here. I had great trepidation about moving home. There was a story with my
mother that needed to be healed. It was---And then there's the ongoing colonizing by the
evangelicals or fundamentalists who control the state and continue to gain control of our
tribes. That rigidity is so difficult to handle. It is an impossible balancing act. The story
of the land theft and the continued legacy of racism also need healing.*

What does Colorado give you that Oklahoma can't, besides mountains?

Linda--What lies beneath my work is a sense that I want and need to make
this one brief life matter in ways that are not about myself so much as
an offering to the world, such as a prayer, a ceremony, a song, a giveaway.
My heart wants to make this whole sentient earth and all its lives available
to those who know it but haven't yet felt or seen it. I love to write and to
write in any genre. A day without writing is like a day without smudging.
It doesn't feel right. It doesn't have the same spirit. Soon I become a little
unsettled. The world feels off kilter.But there are many days not spent
writing because they are days earning a living, doing chores, or other things
that life requires. Still, always there is this requirement of the soul, an urge

to put words down even if they are merely disorganized words.

As for Oklahoma, I listened to pit bull fights from the windows at night and couldn't shut out the sounds. At first I turned them in. The next day my own dog was missing, as were five other "bait" dogs. There were cock fights. There was corruption. I began to feel like I had been home to experience the same things my relatives had been through, and I did finally lose my home, land, place, and all the rest. As my grandfather had done.

The SE region is strong on Christianity. As one of my friends said, Every other man is a preacher. But there were more churches than homes. I was not a member of a church. The first thing people asked was, What church do you go to? The Catholic church had been burned down, by the way. The colonization of our people beg, oan so very early, with the wars starting in the Southeastern part of the continent in the 1500's. We were the ones who sent De Soto away. But we had advance warning of what they had done elsewhere and so were kind to them for a year, planning. One night we shot arrows into their homes (our own) and after that we had learned to use other weapons and won many wars, but also were sold into slavery in the West Indies. Then moved to a new location. Then came the many settlers. Then removal. Civil war. The Dawes Act. More corruption and loss of homes. And so on. And all the history made the people into a different kind than say, Navajo, Lakota, or others who were reached later and had different histories. I wanted to write about our future. I wanted us to return to what we had been when we were whole.

You can't always have things the way you want. But writing it into existence creates a possibility.

As for my inner self, it also is a guide and knows what I don't. I have to follow her. But she is also the line of people I have come from. The women. Their names, the long list. They tell me things to say and write and speak to me. I am only their voice. It is the voice of a wisdom I wish existed in my own daily life, but they are particular about appearing in the work. I think being indigenous also offer the ancient and eco-voice of the land, here, there, and along the Tombigbee.

Still, Colorado offers me more community and it gives me the perfect environment, ancient trees no one is cutting down for cattle ranching, a focus on life, a lack of cruelty. It offers the mountain canyon where I live and a creek running year round. But it takes away house space and warmth for my place is tiny and cold. But I consider my home the wildlife corridor where I live and encounter mountain lions, wolves, bear, and bugling elk. How could I not be happy there? How could I not be grateful that I don't hear suffering at night?

What I learned from birds, having one as a grandmother, was how to be quiet and calm and behave in their presence. How to love all beings and know each one has its own consciousness. It was the healing teachings. I learned from a true healer. Vet schools would send in a killer eagle and then she, Sigrid, would pick it up, no leather glove, and it would be calm, gentle. We could spread its great wing, see where it had been hurt. I learned their love. They taught me that I had to write about what is happening in the environment. Lead poisoning, what it does. Viruses like West Nile. Pain. The cruelty and sometimes ignorance of humans, however unintended. And we learned it from her. She had been a friend/sister to me back when she had only one owl, then somehow we ended up with great flight cages, two intensive care units, a lab, a feed building, and numerous other buildings. It was amazing how it grew. And I wrote about my grandmother, the golden.

But all in all, I write because I love it. I miss a day of it and feel the loss. I would be so happy to write more and work less. Wouldn't you? I mean, do you work at a job? Jobs? How do you live as a writer and musician?

Yes, I try to write daily, even when I am working at another job. As I said, without it, I feel a loss.

Tell me more about how you live and what is around you that strengthens and initiates your work?

Joy--*Most mornings I wake up with a cache of dreams that I unload for meaning. I like to write them down, mine them through the day. The meanings often surface later, and some of them don't make sense in and of themselves, they are small islands of meaning, sometimes profound, often mundane, like a diaper change of a baby. I don't usually dream of diaper changes. I have never had a baby diaper changed in my writing/music room, but there, the day after the dream, my step granddaughter laid her boy down, as his brother who is five and I jammed out on the bass and saxophone. He was going for it on the E string as I showed him. Then, the youngest brother who is about two jumped up from his diaper changed, turned his long baton shaped bubble maker into a soprano saxophone and pretended to blow it and danced in perfect rhythm. What happiness---*

And that was a very small island of meaning, of deep meaning. It wasn't obvious.

Most of all I like to go into silence first, to listen to what I need to know. This morning I had to deal with appointments, bills, planning, and prepping for flying out Thursday for NM. I had to write a poem I promised dealing with a certain form. I decided to combine that with a song I am working on with my old Poetic Justice band mate, John Williams. I wanted to have it done but it's not done—I keep going back to it, crafting it.

And now I have to leave for errands and working out. Tonight after cooking dinner for my beloved and me (he cooks for me too), I will work on the presentation which involves making songs of poetry and the poem and work my saxophone(s)---

Then go out to the stars for a bit to remember how deep they are in us.

Feels like I have to fight for time. It is eaten by obligations. And these days the Internet and our cellphones will eat up the rest of it easily, gulp it—then what do you have to show for it. Any shift of meaning starts from within--- If I am calm and deep I can see. You cannot see through to the bottom in stirred up waters. And what motivates me is to hear, see, and know as deep as possible.

I make my living mostly through traveling to speak and perform. I also have a teaching job of a couple of months a year at the University of Illinois, Urbana-Champaign. At least I think I still have it. I am in the process of trying to move the appointment from one program to another. When I teach it's difficult to continue my writing. My focus is on the students, the art of teaching. Writing is a constant though whatever my obligations. I write music, plays, poetry, memoir, interviews…!.

What has deepened meaning in my life is returning to my ancestral ceremonial grounds. For years I have been involved in the traditional life of my people but I didn't live here. (I was also involved with a different ceremonial ground. It was and remains important to me.)That makes a huge difference. Every season is marked by ceremony. There are things you cannot know or understand until you live it. It is profound and there the ancestors gather.

(I still feel as if I haven't answered the questions. I'll go back over and revise. It's ten p.m. and I still have to rehearse my music, begin to pack, shower, and be ready to get up and leave the house at 7:30 AM for some errands. I'm exhausted right now. I can go into what it takes to do what I/we do—so many have no idea--)

I want to know what you are working on right now. And do you have a vision of what you wish to accomplish before you leave this realm?

Linda--What do I want to accomplish before leaving this realm? I think you mean before leaving this particular lifestream or before I die. When I was in an accident years ago, the ancestors arrived to say that I couldn't leave yet because there was work to be done. They were in the room. I saw a woman in a lavender/purple turban, the kind we once wore (our Chickasaw ancestral clothing)and we talked. My younger daughter and a few others thought I was already one, but I had been taken to a full body MRI. So I feel as if I did leave the realm. I went traveling to other places during that time. I saw splendor in a museum in China, a jade wall. Beautiful visions and sights.

Many years later I had a heart attack and there was the same argument. I had to do something before I could leave. (However, the funny side of this was the long ambulance ride with a tube in my heart from my abdomen. The ambulance played DIXIE for its siren and I wasn't supposed to move, laugh or do anything. They had started surgery but couldn't finish it and had to send me to the city.)

So I will leave when it is time, but what it is that I have left to do doesn't seem to be up to me or to my body. It seems in the hands of the old ones. And I have to follow them. Otherwise I would have left as a child when I used to go outside, look up to where I thought something lived, and say This is enough. I have had it. I don't want to be here. But I never did leave. So here I am, still writing, which had been my accidental art to begin with. I was never in control of the direction I went. I was in psychology and planning to work as a therapist when writing discovered me and became my magical love, my happiness, and my work. Like you, I have not "made a living" from it, but perhaps I have lived for it.

And also, living without a partner means I have to do all the work alone most of the time. Sometimes a friend helps. That is wonderful and I am grateful. But the world and errands are all very demanding and distracting. I do not have the time to do everything and unlike you, I have to neglect inside my home. I have seen how beautifully you live and what surrounds you in your home. However, I am surrounded by the natural world, forest, canyon, and the little cabin is all windows looking out on this amazing and beautiful earth world with deer, with the elk bugling in their season, with also the mountain lions and bear. A wolf pack was there, but I haven't seen them in a long time. And the times I am snowed in are most beautiful and silent. The, spring is the most beautiful with the wildflowers. Then, it is all beauty. So I write about sunrise, the movement of the stars, the way sunlight arrives twice because of the farther peaks of mountains.

But, in the same way as you, whenever I have to pay bills and do other chores, my mind is on writing, and there are many errands and chores. Feeding time for the horse and burro. The burro is an alarm clock, too. She really lets me know the time it is. And then, too, she is a heavy breather. When she sees me come, her excitement for food is so great that she silently brays and makes me laugh. But she can also be somewhat diabolical at times and that makes me laugh, too. My favorite times are when I am still on the bed and watching them run with one another, playing. I write about them often in essays and work I do for journals that are not necessarily about literature.

Which brings me to publication. What do you do to prepare your work, polish it, and make it ready to publish? I have also had Norton for my poetry and do not believe they have done well enough at their publicity. I am somewhat unhappy with both presses now having the book done, but then just ignoring it. What about you?

Oh, yes, you might also mention what your plans are for remaining in this "realm?"

Joy--*I have lived many lives in this one: the enigmatic Indian school theater and painting student, the teenage mother working as a waitress with postponed dreams of being an artist, the young college graduate with an MFA in poetry and her first job teaching at IAIA, published poet, traveler and performer, poet-musician with a band, university professor, activist—I've also raced outrigger canoes in Hawai'i, worked with Healing Touch with horses on a ranch in Waimanalo for a few years, gotten within a few weeks of a weightlifting competition events, jammed on bass with a blues group…*

I always wish I were as prolific and committed as you and others who say that they live to write. I am committed, and once I am in the throes of creation, I am lost in visioning, writing, and rewriting. Then all of the other responsibilities begin to crowd. I have a house to take care of, family responsibilities, a business to run, community responsibilities, a teaching job, and a saxophone that needs my attention. It's a balancing act. I understand the writer who had his family lock him in his room to write, and he escaped. The next time he had them lock him in, nude. Once I'm there, there I am!

I've decided to train myself to include all the responsibilities under the category of "my art", to not see any separation. Of course for a writer, musician, artist…everything is fodder. Maybe each of us is fodder for a larger intelligence.

What I am struck by in your responses is your willingness to admit to your visions, your insight. I noticed that I began to open up more readily and publically around the time I was outed by Leslie Silko in her memoir The Turquoise Ledge as an astrologer. I allowed myself to speak and write more openly of visionary and intuitive experiences. Not long after I published Crazy Brave. I was brazen in many of my revelations in that book. And yet, I held back. One draft version of the memoir was half dreams and visions. My search in this world, my creativity centers on the need to know and express mystery. The deepest motivator is the need for justice.

As a child I lived partially in this world and mostly in the spirit world. Of course, all of this is the spirit world. I'm speaking of a different kind of time and knowing configuration, one in which the ancestors visit and it's natural, not impossible or crazy (in an insane manner). I'm beginning work on my next memoir, researching right now and writing notes. It is centering on indigenous rights movements. I was present at so many events but even as I was present I often felt discounted or invisible and did not always fit myself absolutely in the moment. I will have to take myself back, even plant myself in some memories to see what I can remember, and maybe, what I missed. This is something I am working on now. I think I told myself that I would that I would lose that sense of deep spiritual realms, and the ability to travel through time, if I focused here in the earthly realm. That's just not true. The more aware we are of detail, the deeper our connection to our spirit.

I figure I'll be here for about twenty more years. But who knows---we never truly absolutely know. I have noticed that some people carry a definite, fated timeline, while others have been given, or take more leeway.

As for publishing, there was a huge difference in press attention between publishing a memoir and publishing poetry. With my poetry books the press pretty much depends on my performance schedule to get the word out. With the memoir I went on a book tour in the west. We will see what happens with my next book of poems. This is my first poetry book in about ten years.

Last week was the first time we've performed together in fifteen or twenty years. We'd met up last, I believe, somewhere in Oklahoma. You are as shining and engaged as ever, larg-

er in being though you are smaller. When you read I was struck by how parallel we are in our explorations of consciousness, though the road to knowing differs. I liked watching you with your students. Your life, your words, your poetry… is a testimony of sorts. What has been your most tremendous struggle? And what has brought you the most joy?

Linda--When I saw you, I realized how much I had missed you and remembered you from the 70's in very wild pants and I had never been in such a world as that of writers.

After I returned from hearing you, having always wanted to sing Blues….I came home, tried Garage Band as you suggested, and quickly gave up. My writing called me back. So I will have to sing with the car radio, as usual. I am finishing a novel and have a new book of poems almost ready.

The reason I am committed is because I want to write for this earth, this land so in need of our words and care and love. That is the reason for my commitment, as it was when I was a child and loved the animals and plants.

The ancestors are here with all of us, I think. As you say, we live in a world with their presence. I think of myself as only the in-between for them and the poetry. We speak from the voices of the past for the future.

I know we could continue and keep this conversation going, but maybe this is a good place to stop. We have said the most significant things, I think, and now are talking about our work, like when our parents used to tell us how far they had to go to school…..

I worked in nursing homes, hospitals, dental offices and worked with handicapped children when I first discovered a book of contemporary poetry and began to write. No schooling in literature. By then I was married and I loved my job and the children at the school. Many of them would not live much longer and required a special kind of love. Others would be treated unfairly because of their looks or disabilities. But I also worked full time since the age of fifteen, like you. And then, you were teaching poetry and studying it before I'd heard of it. All I know is I love you and have so many incredible and funny memories of you and have seen your transformation. It has been amazing to watch. But I remember you when you lived in Santa Fe and I drove you home, but the car engine kept freezing and we had to put our hands on it until we found a gas station to buy "Heet." And Rainy and Tanya were about the same age and I baby-sat them while you and Juana went to a wedding. Before that time, we met at Rudolfo Anaya's and you were so cute, laughing and being like a school girl. And then, your life as astrologer, our many meetings at gatherings, places, conferences. You telling me your life. Me probably telling mine. Then your beautiful home in Denver which made me wish for such a home. You come from such a talented family, too, of writers (your mother) and artists and creative people. My family were all musicians. I played, too. But never in public. What I admire is your courage. You have to courage to be on stage in a way that allows you to take risks, so many risks. I would be afraid to sing, to miss a note, so I watch you and listen with an amazement for your ability to have such strength, while I always want to disappear from the microphone, back away, and so I just allow the poems or stories to speak. You love being a performer so much and it is great to watch.

My horses are calling. It is time to go feed. I am late today. I send you warmth and heart and such gratitude.

Love, Linda

Editor's Choice

Charles Eagle Bull

Autobiography

Being born into a land of poverty, life insinuates hardships into the social and daily structure of most people, who cast their lives out to the world hoping to catch a break. Homes are plagued with drunken domestication. Communities are broken into pieces and children learn off of the "lost ones," ones who have stopped traveling the Red Road, to choose a side and to hate the others, for no logical or apparent reasons. The only place growing children can escape the life of domestication on a reservation is in nature itself.

After the split of my parents, my little brother and I bounced between homes that were filled with drunken emotions. Sometimes we did not have a home to go to, just the tiny enclosure of a weathered yellow 1969 Chevy truck. This truck was broken down under a huge cotton wood tree, just below a small steep hill. A worn out tire hung from a mighty branch with a rope that looked like it has seen the world twice. My brother and I used to go on top of the hill with the tire swing and take turns pushing each other off. We had worn out a path with our tiny buffalo like charges up the hill so we could have another go. It was one of the best things to do, besides climbing the huge tree with the help of the tire swing that we wrapped around it. Sitting up on one of the branches and getting to see the land like a bird does is a wonderful thing. This branch has hosted many day dreaming and discussions, between my brother and I, about what bird we would be and why. Where we would go, how high, and we would dramatically make motions with our hands and arms on how we would dive to the earth and swoop back up. Thinking back, I am so happy and thankful that that old cotton wood tree had the patience to put up with our shenanigans and to hear our crazy stories.

After finally moving into a trailer house, of our own, with one of our parents, we still endured the same life style. We just had more laborious work to do. The trailer house was located about half a mile off of the main road. Next to a creek and a pasture full of cows. No electricity. No running water. Just a rusted wood stove and an old water pump that was located 147 yards away. The winters were tough. In order to have drinking water, my brother and I had marched back and forth to the old water pump with five gallon buckets. Sometimes we made that journey through waist deep snow in negative degree weather. I was only in the fourth grade during this time while my brother was in the second. One of our care takers was injured while at work and was unable to do physical activity the whole winter. We helped to get fire wood, and we chopped that wood ourselves, sometimes in blizzards, so our family would not freeze to death. The wood freezes in those kinds of temperatures, and it is very difficult for a fourth grader to split. After we had completed our duties to our family, we went out into the cold and snow. We had these huge puffy snow suits and we re-enacted WWE professional signatures moves, which we learned by visiting grandma during Monday nights, in the thick snows. We had snow ball wars with our very own snow forts, and we conjured countless snow men for our army. During one cold snowy night, we were outside making snow angels and counting the stars. We were so fortunate to see a falling star that left a trail that contained the colors of a bright rainbow. We had the times of our lives out in the snow. I think that is why I am always out in storms and playing in the snow to this day. I can say that I love to walk around in blizzards and in huge thick snowfall.

We had moved back with our other parent to a small border town that was populated by 12 people. The border town, I do not even think it was big enough to be called a town. If you were to blink you might miss it. But people hardly ever missed this place. For it hosted a trading post and a bar. People would stop in to sell items and buy beer and head on back to their homes, or enjoy the bar life, or come to our tiny trailer for a party. This was the night life my brother and I had. We had seen all types of people come through; cowboys, natives, and even had some crazy tourists. During the day we helped with ranch work and care taking of the animals and structures. We learned lessons of a rancher and a cowboy.

In our free time, we ventured off into the Badlands, which we discovered is home to many dangers. We had our fair shares of encounters with rattle snakes and coyotes. The small cactus were also mean to us. Stabbing and jabbing as if they were trying to tell us to turn around. Warning us of unforeseen danger. On top of the Badland buttes, there are holes that go deep into the ground. We would throw rocks down into them and listen to the sound of the rocks disappear, never hearing the crash of the rock against the bottom floor. Those holes are big enough to swallow a small child. We learned to appreciate that Nature is dangerous and not always nice. That it could take our lives just like that. Despite all of the warning and dangers, we still went out every day. We really were not afraid of the dangers that nature had to offer. We respected it.

We moved back with our other parent who had attained a house within a small community. This place was surrounded by large hills that took close to thirty minutes to get to the top of it. The surrounding hills behind were almost untouched. It had this feel about it that it held an image of the old days, before the European age. In this community, gangs were rampant, and every week there was a gang fight. When I was in the fifth grade, I gave into peer pressure and fought, smoked cigarettes, chewed tobacco, wore gang colors, cursed, stole and threw up gang signs. After a period of time, my elder in the gang decided to burn me with a spoon on the arm, instead of the hot butter knife that sliced open caverns into the older ones' skin. This was a sign that showed one's alliance and devotion to the gang. Sometime after this, I was betrayed and was turned on by the very gang members that was supposed to watch over me. I was stronger and a litter older by this time. I fought my way through six of them, only to be attacked by the Rottweiler that belonged to the gang. The scar from him can be seen on my right arm. That dog died during that struggle and even though it attacked me, I felt an overwhelming remorse.

My brother and I would find ourselves in the hills, picking up branches and pretending they were swords. We saved imaginary worlds from many monsters and bad guys. This was our escape. This became our home away from home.

About a month later, we lost our grandma, our father, and grandpa in the same month, in that order. We helped our father bury his mom, then we helped our grandpa bury his son, then my brother and I buried our grandpa. Feeling lost and alone, I went for a walk in my hills, the hills that felt like they preserved the old ways. I did not know what to do, I have cried so many tears, I have been hugged and talked to by so many people and still nothing was helping. So I prayed. I prayed in the way I knew how. I prayed to the old rocks, to the grass and roots that are growing right along with me, to the trees who lived through nature's best and worst, to the small critters and to the mighty buffalo. I prayed for my brother and all the people around me. Asking for the strength to keep going through whatever life decided to throw at me. I no longer felt alone. There was this creeping comfort that didn't really dull the pain. It was just enough. When darkness reached its grasp across the trees and rocks, I came down from the hills feeling a little better. I placed my head down in that old feather pillow, pulled my star quilt over my little brother and I. Then I prepared for whatever else was to come to us and went sleep.

Those hills, rocks, trees, grass, roots and the other nations that live in them is my place of comfort. I do not feel alone out in nature, even though I am all by myself. There is a connection I have with Nature. Not just spiritually, but a sense and respect that we are all trying to live a good life in this world. That we are connected to each other more than one way, and we rely on each other. It is sad that people are oblivious to this fact. Nature is so beautiful and powerful. It contains all the teachings that we all need to know. People just need to take the time to go out and see the world for what it really has to offer besides natural resources. Nature is responsible for most of my knowledge and wisdom about life. The rest is through trial and error and just straight up bad luck.

Amongst the whiskey gladiators and beer kings and queens, there are a few who remember and carried on the teachings that have been passed down through time amongst our people. My grandparents and my friend's elders introduced us to the life of a Lakota. Prayer, compassion, respect, generosity, humility, honesty, and wisdom is what a Lakota stands by. I remember them telling us that it is a difficult life to live. We have to walk in two worlds. The domesticated life of Europeans and the life of our people. Amongst the many teachings of our responsibility in society, we also were taught the prayer life of Lakota.

Amongst all the negativity, darkness, and despair there lies faith. But it is not an easy thing to find, this faith. Best way I can explain the situation to finding faith is like a small candle light in a dark heavy fog. People wonder aimlessly and some are lucky to find it. I have seen things on my reservation. Good turn to bad, bad turn to good, people falling like a burning building, and I have seen people rise from the ashes. There are leaders amongst the reservation that help people back onto Canku Luta, the Red Road. The life of a Lakota. Spiritual leaders take on the burden of keeping the people together and being the light in the dark. People are starting to finally come together as Lakota people to solve the problems that plague our communities. I am very happy to see these actions that people are starting to make. Maybe one day we all can stand together as a nation and continue to grow and help people with struggles. Also keeping our respect and duties to nature. I try to teach my sisters and their friends what Mother Nature has taught me. I take them on walks and teach them the dangers and the life that belongs to nature. To walk with respect for everything around us and to pray for strength to be strong for those who are weak. My beautiful and strong mother quit drinking, went back to school, received an education and is a very well recognized counselor amongst our tribal College. She is my inspiration and hero.

Mother Nature is our beginning and our end. We are a part of her just as much as she is a part of us. I will forever have a special place amongst the other nations of the world. They will always have a special place within me. For I found my connection amongst them.

Rick DeMarinis Short Story Prize: 1st Place

Chosen by Bobbie Ann Mason

Aleksey Babyev

Top of the Morning

"Off to the pub then are ya?"

The lady from the eighth floor steals a nervous glance at me and the baby. Say it isn't so, it seems to beg. Who takes a baby to the pub at nine in the morning? On a Saturday?

We've just shared an elevator ride. I feel obliged to reassure her.

"No, Teddy," I say, coldly, to the concierge. "Not this morning."

The lady hurries out the front door of our luxury high-rise. We stick around so that I can force Tomcat into her coat.

"No?" Teddy hovers above the stroller. "No pub today for Daddy? Who's not letting Daddy have his morning pint?"

Tomcat smiles with her entire face, as if Teddy were the epitome of things wondrous and hilarious.

"Is it Baby? No! Is it? No! Baby's not letting Daddy have his morning pint! His morning

pint and his morning football!"

I don't know what it is about Teddy's *Irishness* that makes it more okay for me to have him as my concierge. Something in that accent doesn't offend my Soviet upbringing quite so much. We weren't supposed to have servants, growing up. I like to think there's something about *my* Russian accent that makes it more bearable for Teddy to be my concierge. Still, we need to have a word about that *familiarity* in front of the neighbors—must everyone in the building know about our pub habits? Not to point fingers, but my people didn't invent the whole "take the baby down the pub" thing. Can we agree to speak easy on the topic? "Don't tell me the score now!" he wags his finger as he holds open the door for us. "I'm taping it!"

Lately, our Saturday routine has been Dunkin Donuts—East River—Farmers' market. And yes, the baby and I visit the pub on occasion. I don't know what the big deal is.

At Dunkin, I get coffee while Tomcat flirts with the customers. Today I also get a Boston Cream. Daddy's reward for being out so early. What the hell—make that two Boston Creams. Daddy only lives once. I pay with a card to keep my hands clean for Tomcat.

"*Oh. My. God.*" I hear a woman's voice from the line behind. This is usually how it begins. I stuff the donuts into the diaper bag and turn around.

"*She is beautiful!*"

The woman is your typical Upper East Side Dunkin weekend morning customer: long gray hair, black oversized jacket, shiny Louis Vuitton bag.

"Thank you."

"Those eyes!"

"Thank you."

"How old?"

"Ten months."

"And will you just look at that fancy *strollah!*"

A disheveled kid in a Michigan State fleece steps out of the line to shake his head in appreciation. "Sweet ride man!"

I know. In our family, the stroller is an item of particular pride. It is orange and Scandinavian. It is minimalist and stealthy. It looks like it's about to fly off.

Tomcat bares her two bottom teeth—her only two teeth—and graces the line with cheerful drooling.

"Gggggggg wooooooo. Aaaaooo."

"I'm going to die this baby's so cute," concludes the woman.

I consider this a good stopping point and make for the door.

"Bye-bye pumpkin! Bye-bye little princess!"

"Byeeee."

"Young man?" I hear from a nearby table. Two construction workers, one around my

age, the other maybe a decade older.

"Yes?"

"Do you speak English?" asks the older one.

I decide to take that as a compliment, as in we look so *continentally dashing* this morning.

"*Oui..* I do."

"Yeah? Okay. This young man here, you see," he points at the younger one, "is a father-to-be. He was kind of wondering about your stroller."

"Congratulations," I say. "What about the stroller?"

"How much would you say a stroller like that would set him back? He was just wondering."

I mean to tell them what we paid for it last year—but add, for some reason, another thousand. They burst out laughing.

"Let me ask you something," says the older guy. "When you need it in the morning—

do you just whistle?"

"Radio on it?" asks the younger guy.

"No radio."

"Take care of that baby," says the older one.

Outside, I unsnap Tomcat's seat from the base, turn it around to face me, snap it back in, tilt it forward and slide it up along the base. Tomcat is now sitting at eye level. We pause to smile at each other: worldly mechanic to rookie pilot. Shall we take this bébé for a spin? I shift le machine ninety de-grees with a sleight of the left hand—the coffee occupying my right—hand Tomcat her stuffed pink lion, and we head uptown.

Three sips of the coffee, I get the rush. The *today, I will finally conquer the world* rush. Tomcat is with me on this—she slaps her puffy palms on the mid-seat bar, casts aside the stuffed pink lion and makes her favorite inhaling sound, like she's just discovered the wind and will continue to be surprised by it every few seconds, indefinitely. "*Moya kisya*," I say to her. My Little Cat. "*Kisya sladkii Kot!*" Little Cat - sweet Tomcat! We pass everyone on the street. Most people act like they've never been passed by a stroller before—sorry. I walk fast. I walk even faster with a stroller, because it's got premium wheels. And did I mention that inside the stroller is my very own girl, all eyelashes and tiny toes, who loves a fast ride? My girl! What Russian doesn't love a fast ride? Not Tomcat. Kindly move out of the way.

We drop a DVD into the return box of a video store on the corner of Eighty-second (*Last Tango in Paris*, from last night, Cultural Fridays we call it now that we don't go out anymore.) We check the score from outside a bar on the corner of Eightythird—Teddy's team is up 1-0. We cross the avenue at Eighty-fourth and head for the river.

Halfway down the deserted Eighty-fourth, Tomcat tries to untangle herself from her scarf. In the Western world, they tell you to imagine how much you would wear when dressing your baby, then add a layer. The Russian school prescribes seven additional layers and a blanket. Tomcat and I are always unwrapping—I figure that as the ultimate winners in the Russians' millennium-old war against the cold, we have that right. We no longer have to conserve energy to hunt seal in the morning. Our young will not (I knock three times on the nearest wooden handrail) get pneumonia simply from being outside. I unbutton Tomcat's coat, take off the scarf, and remove the blanket. I roll up the sleeves of the coat and roll my sleeves up, too. Today, we will conquer the world together.

"What is autumn? Sky is autumn," I sing to Tomcat in Russian. "Sky, weeping sky on the ground. In puddles we see images of some birds and clouds. Autumn, it's been a while since I was with you." My voice is hoarse from last night's Cultural Friday. We drank two bottles of wine and wolfed down a pack of Parliaments during Last Tango. That is how you watch this movie, my wife said. Tomcat is looking up, anticipating my next move. Will I sing more? Walk even faster? Tickle her with my scruffy face? Whatever it is, it is going to be fantastic. A day will come when I'm not dad enough to protect her from disappointment.

On the playground at Carl Schurz Park, Tomcat dangles in the infant swing while I gulp down the donuts and scope out the competition. We've got a whimpering blond two year-old swinging over to the left and a skinny girl about Tomcat's age to the right. The girl tries to get our attention, but Tomcat is busy throwing exploratory smiles at the boy, who is brazenly uninterested. His exhausted-looking mom is rocking the swing as if she wants him to go to sleep. Not on our watch. It is Showtime.

I grab Tomcat's swing abruptly, pull it up as high as I can, pause for a split second to smile into Tomcat's widening face, and let go. The amplitude is an infant swing record. What Russian doesn't love a good swing? Tomcat drops her tiny jaw and giggles as she flies away. Ground Control to First Baby in Space: who is the cutest astronaut of all time? We swing in this vaudevillian fashion long enough to force the also-rans and their parents to stop and watch, unable or unwilling to compete. That is how you swing, boys and girls. When it's time to leave, Tomcat cries.

She won't go back into the stroller, so I carry her to our second stop: the small dog run, where small dogs skid after tennis balls in a tiled oval-shaped enclosure the size of a large studio. I let Tomcat hang on to the railing and tell her to look at the doggie! look at the doggie! not referring to any one doggie but rather doggie as a concept. She howls impatiently until a little white poodle with a heart-shaped tag runs straight at us and places its front paws on the border of the fence. Before I can react, Tomcat's hands have been licked.

A pretty red-haired girl in running clothes rushes over to us and picks up the dog. "I'm so sorry," she says. "This is Lola. She loves babies."
"No problem," I say, even though I'm not sure what to do with Tomcat's hands now—what if she puts them in her mouth and gets rabies? "This is Tomcat. She is interested in dogs."
"It's good to get them started early," says the girl. "I can always tell a dog person on the street."
"We are not dog people yet," I tell her. "But we are working on it."

The girl smiles and they leave, but as I'm prepping Tomcat for disinfection procedures they reappear, having come out of the enclosure to say hello. I hold up Tomcat and the girl holds up Lola so that their noses almost touch. "She won't bite," says the girl.
"Will you say hello to Lola?" I say to Tomcat in English, which startles her. "Look at Lola! Lola is a dog."
I don't know what to say to get this over with; I don't want anyone to think that I'm hitting on the girl while I'm with Tomcat.
"Isn't Lola the cutest?" I prod Tomcat. "Sort of like the squirrel we saw yesterday in the park, remember? Except even furrier."
"You guys are so cute."
"Thank you," I say, avoiding the girl's eyes. "So are you. You guys, I mean."
I wonder if I've gone too far. It's easy enough to say the wrong thing to an American girl when not holding a baby in your hands.
"How old is she?"
"Ten months."
"Your first child?"
"Yeah."
I'm probably supposed to ask about Lola, but I let the scene expire.
"Well," says the girl. "See you!"
"Byeeee."

The encounter has visibly exhausted Tomcat. I wipe her hands with a whole stack of wet wipes and cover her with a blanket. We start gliding down the promenade along the river: Roosevelt Island to our left, FDR Drive below, red-brick condominiums to the right. Queensboro Bridge afore and Triboro

Bridge astern. This is the America I imagined back in Russia: tall, steely, cloudy, mean. A place where a man of substance and his infant daughter could proudly stroll. Tomcat was born fourteen blocks down, on Sixty-eighth street—our maternity ward room had the exact same river view.

We haven't reached our last stop in the park, so I keep Tomcat awake with another Russian song about autumn, duck hunting, and fleeting luck. "Once more autumn has stirred up a carousel of sounds... What a shot—alas, I'm not the lucky one... I don't care that I'm often living day-to-day! I just know it: it's going to come back to me. It will absolutely all come back to me! Hunting weather, hope, and my friends' embrace..."

I finish the song and we come to the edge of the promenade, which becomes an overpass above FDR. I lean the stroller against the railing, tilt the seat forward and let Tomcat direct traffic from above. She grabs the mid-seat bar like it's a handlebar on a bike and shakes the carriage back and forth. "Look at the cars!" I tell her. "Look at the cars sweetie!" We've got an open view of the river, the drive, the bridge, and the stately terracotta manors lining the highway for twenty blocks down. A woman smoking on a corner balcony of a building just ahead of us waves hello. The wind blows through us from all directions. I recline the seat back, hand Tomcat her pink pacifier, and we make our exit onto the street.

When my rambling story, begun with "once upon a time, Tomcat and Daddy went to the zoo" finishes, five minutes later, with "and then, everybody had peach macaroons!" Tomcat's eyelids are half-closed. Yeah: other men in my family have done real, manly things. Fought in wars, built furniture, moved households across continents, powered by nothing more than a desire for a better life and a hundred grams of vodka before bed. I haven't had to be like them. But I tell a mean bedtime story—different every time except for the peach macaroons. No way those guys were doing that. I bet I walk faster than them, too: we power-stroll into the warm autumn breeze, yellow and orange leaves deliciously cracking under our wheels.

Tomcat has just fallen asleep when we get to the Farmers' Market on Eighty-second street, in the courtyard of St. Stephen's of Hungary. Stern Hungarian ladies sell rice cakes and sugar crepes outside the gate. Inside the small tree-lined courtyard there is a vegetable stand, a bread stand, and a fresh fish tent in the back. We've bought fresh fish here the past two Saturdays.

The tent is manned by a tall guy in a filthy white hoodie and a chubby girl in a New Hampshire fleece (I've decided that they are siblings.) They look a bit out of place here, between a pensive statue of the Virgin and an entrance to something called Boys Rectory. The girl has dark brown eyes and an uneven complexion. The guy bears a passing resemblance to Harry Connick Jr.

"How can I help you, boss?"

"Yeah," I say. "Listen. We got tile fish here last time—not sure what happened but it made us sick. Don't know if I kept it out too long, or didn't cook it right away, or maybe it wasn't fresh enough or something... Anyone else say anything?"

"About the tile fish? Don't think so man. Hey," he says to the girl, who's moving something from cooler to cooler in the back of the tent, "did anyone complain about the tile fish last week?"

"Never heard of anyone complaining," she answers without turning around.

"You probably kept it out too long," he says. "I'll get you an ice pack today. And better not wait until the next day. It's best when it's fresh, you know what I'm saying?"

"All right," I say and check out the plastic containers on display, as if I know anything about fish. "The bass looks good. I'll try the bass today. A pound and a quarter of bass."

"Nice. You know what you're gonna do with it?"

"I will probably grill it," I say with some hesitation, as if weighing my options. "On an indoor grill."

"Nice," he nods. "Spray it with some lemon and stuff. You're gonna love it."

He opens the container with the striped bass but doesn't take from the top layer. Instead he reaches into the middle, grabs two pieces, and quickly slaps them on some wrapping paper on the scales.

"Can I see that bass again?" I ask.

"What?" he says, surprised. "See it? Here."

"It's a different color, man," I say. "It's a different color from the ones on the top."

"A different color?"

"Look," I say. "My daughter is just starting to eat normal food. We were thinking about getting her to try some fish this weekend. I don't want her to get sick from it."

"What are you saying?"

I shrug and take a look around. There is a short bald middle-aged guy at the other end of the row of containers, asking the girl about scallops. He is the only other customer here. The two other stands are nearly empty as well. The market is closing. Tomcat is sleeping. We're deep inside the courtyard. I want to leave.

Instead, I tell Harry Connick: "Look. I just don't want her to get sick from the fish."
"Hold on," he says. "You're saying I sell bad fish? Is that what you're saying?"
The girl and the bald guy stop their conversation to look at us.
"I have no idea," I say. "I just want the bright, pinkish fish from the top of the container, not the darker fish from the middle."
"Pinkish?" he laughs. The girl laughs too, revealing big yellow teeth. "Bass ain't 'pinkish,' my friend. Dark stripes, silvery body. Look here," his massive calloused hand takes a piece from the top of the pile and dangles it in front of my face. "This is the fish you want? This is the fish you want? Take it and get out of here."
The middle-aged bald guy hurriedly pays for the scallops and skips away.
"What?" I say, dumbfounded.
"I said do me a favor and get the fuck out of here." He throws another piece of fish on top of the first one and quickly wraps them up. "That should be a pound and a quarter. My fucking gift—to you." He slides the package along the counter, goes to the other end of the tent and takes a swig from an open jug of water. He then gives me a red-eyed look and starts counting cash from the register. The girl disappears behind the tent.

I search for the proper reaction because I don't know what to do. I mean, I do know: we should leave. I will buy my fish at the gourmet store for five more dollars a pound and make an adjustment to our routine for next Saturday.
But I will not be talked to like this—not in front of my daughter. Not in our neighborhood.
"Do me a favor," I say after a pause.
He looks up. "You still here, pinkface?"
"Still here man."
"Yeah? And?"
"Do me a favor. Don't let your ugly-ass sister near this place again. She gives me the fucking creeps."
I somehow know he won't do or say anything more, so I calmly take the stroller off the footbrake, unclench my back, and slowly exit the courtyard

.

Outside, the adrenaline wears off, and I begin to feel terrible. Mainly about endangering Tomcat, but also about the fishmonger's sister. What did she ever do to me? I'm not even certain it was the fish that made us sick last week. Was it even last week? I don't feel bad for Harry Connick though—what country does he think this is? This is a premium zip code buddy. I'm dying for a cigarette, but I don't smoke in front of Tomcat. I look at my cell phone—10:45. We've got another forty-five minutes before we have to be home for the second feeding. We usually use this time to stock up on baby food and diapers.

Tomcat is still sleeping when we get to the pub. I park in the alcove near the door and sit at the bar. The match has just ended. I lived around the corner from this place when I first came to New York. After September 11th, I was in here every night for four months.

"Top of the morning to you Pauline!" I greet the barkeep. "United win?"
"Three-nil," says Pauline. "And how's the little lady?"
"She's had quite a walk," I say. "She'll have the Irish Car Bomb."
"Not too early for the Car Bomb, love?"
I often think about fixing Pauline up with Teddy.

"Did you know," chimes in an old English guy in a Sunderland scarf—the team that has just lost, "that in some states it is illegal to drink and then drive a baby carriage?"
"Sure," I nod. "In some states."

Rick DeMarinis Short Story Prize: 2nd Place

Chosen by Bobbie Ann Mason

Jacob Appel
Thorns For The Negro

The other thing I done when Emily Grierson died was make myself scarce. Nothing good comes from an old Negro haunting about a white woman's house, dead nor alive, even if he's been sleeping under her roof since her father, Master Jonas, bought him at auction in Natchez when he was half the height of a hitching post. Soon enough, folks grow full of suspicions—start counting silver, cry bloody murder over missing candlesticks that ain't been laid eyes upon since Moses parted the Red Sea or thereabouts. And that's how Doc Tobe gonna end up strange fruit hanging off a high branch, as they call it, which ain't God's plan, I reckon, and certainly ain't Doc Tobe's. So I opened the front door for the first of those mourning ladies, them a gaggle of muslin and taffeta, me all shuffles and grins, and then I took my Gladstone—what was once Master Jonas' bag—and I walked straight through the Grierson foyer, and down the pantry stairs, and that's the last Yoknapatawpha County ever done see of yours truly, thank ye very much.

Not that those pasty ladies and their oily-round husbands have no truck calling themselves mourners. Buzzards, more like. Waiting for poor Emily to meet the Almighty so they could go a-poking and a-prodding in her cupboards, underneath her shelving paper, satisfying their curiosities on a diet of somebody else's business. Shameless buzzards. And not one of them folks coming about for a good thirty years before, unless it was to dun the homeowner over taxes or bedevil her with some new ordinance, like that time they tried to nail a metal letterbox to the door. Young-fangled judges and aldermen and constables, all thinking their notions best, when we done just fine the old way. Poor lady ain't conducted correspondence in half a lifetime—not so much as a penny postcard. So what in tarnation, I ask you, does she need with a postbox?

Wasn't always like this, of course. Was a time when I was a lad, and Emily a mere babe, when the grandfathers of them young-fangled judges and alderman smoked together in the drawing room with Master Jonas, talking cotton and horses and politics, while Emily's mama and her Aunt

Jeanie—that was soon married to Colonel Sartoris' son and later drowned down at Mobile—yes, the pair of them Wyatt sisters baled in whalebone, gossiped the very ears off the mothers and grandmothers of those same women who came to mourn their kin. One of those hot summer evenings was when things got to be started between me and Emily, or at least started on the path of how they ended up, though she couldn't have been none more than eight or nine years old.

There was a dozen of us serving folks at the house in those days, but the rest of them lived in the cedar shacks out back, except Ruby and me, who shared a sloping corner of attic opposite the chimneys. Ruby's been gone half a century, if it's been a day—carried off in the second wave of yellow jack—but no mortal before nor since ever fixed a Brunswick stew to make the mouth water like she done. Rumor had it that a merchant from Hattiesburg once tasted her buttermilk pie and offered Master Jonas four thousand dollars in gold for her on the spot, which I have no cause to doubt. She was a stout, kindly woman, probably in her thirties, but she seemed very much older, and Emily, as an only child, had taken a shine to her. They had a routine going, those two: Ruby had rigged herself what's called a Georgia bed, this one-legged contraption built straight into the attic wall, and Miss Emily—for that's what I called her back then—made a habit of stowing herself under the planks and charging Ruby a "nighttime story" to crawl out. Only that particularly night was an engagement party for one of Master Jonas's business associates, and Ruby was late airing out the kitchen, so I came up to my pallet and found myself alone with Miss Emily.

She peered out from the shadows, her skirt fanned around her knees. Even then she had a doughy, lopsided look—like a husk doll fashioned from blighted corn.

"Do you want to marry someday, Tobe?" she asked.

I'd been on my feet since daybreak, serving and hauling, and was in no frame of mind for conversation. "Haven't thought about it too much, Miss Emily," I said, stretching out my bones on the straw. "Not one way or another."

That wasn't exactly true. There was this butter-skinned girl in a kitchen up the alley—easy on the eyes, despite a mean limp—who I'd been intending to make acquaintances with. But that was nothing to be sharing with Miss Emily.

"I want to marry someday," she announced—as though she'd been challenged. "Well, Tobe? What do you think of that?"

"I think that's a right fine idea, Miss Emily," I said.

"And do you know *who* I want to marry?"

"Can't say I do," I said.

"I want to marry *you*, Tobe. What do you think of *that?*"

Rattle of a pygmy snake couldn't have cleared my head quicker.

"I think that's a foolish thing to be saying. Even for a little girl."

Miss Emily folded her arms across her chest. "It'll serve them all right."

The pit of my stomach opened up: That was the sort of talk that saw a fellow whipped or sold down river or worse, but I couldn't come out and tell her not to say such things neither, because that would sound like I was taking her seriously.

"Don't worry. I won't tell anyone," said Miss Emily. "It's our secret."

And then Ruby trundled over the threshold, crooning a hymn under her breath, and that was the last of that nonsense, or so I believed.

~

The years soon took a toll on Master Jonas. I never could get my mind around how the Griersons paid their bills; the family claimed to trade in sweet potatoes one day and Indian corn the next, and rumor had it that Master Jonas also owned interests in a patent distillery and a pair of clipper ships and a dry goods outfit on High Street in Natchez, but whatever enterprise it was keeping Emily's mama and her gigglish aunts in Venetian satins and French perfumes, bills were going unpaid long before the war broke out. By then, Mistress Anne was dead with the typhoid, and Master Jonas smelled of bourbon at midday, passed his afternoons snuffing on the settee in his departed wife's sitting room, cursing the newspapers like they was carriage horses gone lame, and by nightfall the man stank of death itself, while Emily was a ripe young lady of eighteen, waited for a suitor.

A few beaus did come round in the early months of the war—"muster up and marry" seemed to be the refrain of the season— but Emily, for all she was plump as a quail and downright sallow, turned them boys out, one after another, like so many unwanted curs. That left us Negroes scratching our heads, because you'd have thought a young lady in her place would have jumped at any fitting proposal, even if she hadn't been nearly-orphaned and half-bankrupt. I did catch her glancing at me, from time to time, her coal-black eyes savagely a-flicker, but though I hadn't forgotten what had passed between us that evening in the attic, I promised myself it was just my fancy playing tricks on me. Not that I wasn't a respectable looking fellow, if I do say so myself, but there's a wide gulf between what a nine-year-old child wishes and what a sixteen-year-old woman knows to be possible. And then one day the war was long over, and Master Jonas was in the ground at least a fortnight, and it was just me and Emily, alone in the parlor where her father had once played cribbage with judges and senators. That was after the apoplexy carried off Old Canna, and her daughter done vanished, and I was the only Negro left residing on the premises.

Emily had drawn an Ottoman alongside the fire screen, feet from the coffin door which her parents had passed through on the way to Glory. It was early spring; the newly-polished pokers gleamed in their stand by the hearth. I'd brewed her a cup of tea and stood waiting for further instructions, part of me fearing that she might dismiss me for good, maybe shutter the house and take lodgings with her spinster cousins in Alabama. Emily looked at me, her face all brow and chin, her deep-set eyes black as the jaspers in Master Jonas's cufflinks.

"Well, Tobe," she said. "I never thought we'd be rid of those hens. A person can only take so much clucking in one lifetime."

It took me a moment to see she meant her father's mourners.

"Yes, Miss Emily," I said.

"Now we can finally talk." She sat splay-legged on the Ottoman, her petticoats riding miles up her swollen ankles. "Will you sit down? How am I supposed to talk to a man twice my height when he's standing up?"

I looked about the room and half-rested my haunch on the arm of the sofa.

"That's better," declared Emily. "Now we see each other eye to eye."

She locked her gaze on mine and I didn't dare look away. "Do you know what I'd like for us to talk about?" she asked.

"Daresay I don't, Miss Emily."

"I suspect you probably do," she said. "But no matter. What I have to say is that it's not fitting for a man and woman like you and me to be living under the same roof together at the same time, with no other kinfolk, unless they're living as man and wife…."

"I'm not sure I understand, Miss Emily," I said. "Are you telling me to leave you be?"

A faint smile spread across her thin lips. "That's not at all what I'm saying…."

Outside, the sun was already dipping behind the hills, and a gray silence fell over the room, fast like a rustler dropping off a gallows. From the porch next door came the tune of a harmonica, the muffled notes breaking against the bay windows. I wasn't sure what to say, and then I done noticed that Emily's hand was a-trembling, fingers shaking as though she was having the fits, and I saw she was more scared than me. Terrified. Still, I weighed my options: Emily was a white woman, and she was none too pretty, and none too rich neither, anymore, while I was a free man—or so Mr. Lincoln had said before they butchered him—which gave me every right to make my own decisions, and I was set on choosing wise and careful. But I did my calculations, and re-calculations—planning out a whole series of possible lifetimes in less time that it took the tall-case clock to tick off a minute—and I saw I didn't have much choice at all.

"Now I understand what you're saying, Miss Emily," I said.

And I flashed my teeth. And her smile broadened. And somehow I found myself with my hands wrapped around her rump and my eyes only inches from hers.

"You're going to have to stop calling me 'Miss Emily,'" she said.

"I don't know if I can do that."

"Then I'm going to start calling you Master Tobe," she replied. "Or better yet, Doc Tobe. You look smart, you know. Like a doctor." She paused, and for an instant I feared she was going to tell me the whole business was in jest, but she didn't. Instead, she laughed—first time I reckon I ever heard her laugh—shrill and a tad wild. "Can you imagine what Papa would say if he heard me calling one of his Negros 'Doc Tobe'?"

That was the moment I saw how much she'd hated her father all those years, though months would pass before she told me how Master Jonas had been familiar with her. Overly familiar, if you take my meaning. And not only when he was drinking.

Emily cut her hair short that evening, sheared her locks down near to the very scalp. "To look like a Negro wench," she said. "So you'll feel more comfortable." To this day, I'm still not certain if she was joking. Later, when I tried to carry her into her bed chamber, she ordered me up the stairs—and from that night on, both of us slept on the straw pallet in the attic.

~

That was about the time they started laying the sidewalks in Jefferson, and they brought in crews of young Negroes from as far away as Memphis and Cincinnati, Ohio. I got to talking with some of those bucks while I was walking to the market, and one of them fellows planted in my head the notion of sailing to France. Negroes had been free forever in France, or at least since Emperor Napoleon; that fellow didn't know anyone who'd been there himself, but he'd overheard some white folks discussing the place, and he were sure it were true. I'd go, he said—beaming, like he was talking about crossing the Jordan—*if I wasn't so afeared of the water.*

"Just think of that," I said to Emily. "No hiding and pretending. You and I could walk down the main street together like we was king and queen of France."

She shooed off my plan with the back of her hand. "Don't you go believing everything you hear from Negroes on the streets." She fanned herself vigorously, fighting off the heat and the black flies. "Trust me. Everyplace is just like everyplace else."

I cleared my throat. "But folks are starting to talk...."

"Are they?"

"Saying you ain't right in the head since Master Jonas died."

Emily laughed—very near a cackle. "Am I? I'm keeping house with a Negro, and I'm not going to church, and I haven't answered any of those forsaken sympathy cards. So maybe they do need to send me off to Milledgeville like Crazy Aunt Wyatt."

"Nothing good comes of folks talking," I said.

That set her a-thinking. What made Emily different from most white folks was that she heard you when you spoke to her, even if you were a Negro, or a cripple, or one of the mackerel tabbies lurking behind the kitchen. She listened— maybe because she knew what it was like not to be listened to, growing up all those years with Mistress Anne ignoring her and Master Jonas shouting his head off like blood murder. Suddenly, she set down her fan. "You're right there, Tobe. Nothing good ever comes from gossip."

"It's only whispers now," I said. "But it's easier to poison pups than wolves."

"Very well. You've convinced me," she said. "I'll take care of it."

And that was how, less than a week later, she came to be having afternoon tea with that hot-faced Yankee foreman, Homer Barron.

Arm in arm the two of them appeared, and the Yankee settled onto one of Master Jonas' high-backed chairs and lit a cigar like he owned the place. Put his work boots up on one of Mistress Anne's embroidered hassocks. "Boy," he ordered, "Get me a whiskey."

"I admire a man who can hold his liquor," said Emily.

I sensed the rage boiling inside me, not merely because I'd forgotten, ever since Master Jonas's death, what it felt like to be commanded about, but because Emily was all a-titter over the foreman's yarns—vulgar anecdotes salted with crass humor. The Yankee had the habit of slapping his own thigh to punctuate his jokes, and without fail, the instant his palm hit his trousers, Emily started chortling like a jackal. I like near grabbed the pistol from Homer Barron's holster and shot the three of us, that's how sizzled up I was.

After two swigs of whiskey, our guest decided the liquor wasn't strong enough for him and sent me to the cellar for some rum. I was climbing back upstairs, candle in one hand and a cask of bumbo in the other, when Emily appeared at the railing. "Well? What do you think of the enchanting Homer Baron?" she asked.

I kept my rage to a mutter and my head down.

"What's that?" demanded Emily. "You're not jealous, are you?"

"Glory be. You are jealous," she said in a softer voice. "Now isn't that flattering."

The steps creaked under my shoes. "Glad you're amused," I said.

"Look here, Tobe," she exclaimed, grabbing my arm. "You've got nothing to be afraid of with Homer Barron. You can trust me to the bank on that."

I shook her off. "Could have fooled me."

"Good. That's the point," said Emily. "Alas, our Yankee friend prefers the company of gentlemen to that of ladies. Particularly younger gentleman."

I was slow to take her meaning. "You mean something unnatural like?"

"Sure do," said Emily. "I've never seen a man's eyes open so wide as his do when those boys of his perspire through their singlets."

From the parlor came the sound of Homer Barron shouting for his drink.

"And what's to be gained from inviting this man for tea?" I asked.

"I'm going to make him a proposal," said Emily. "You want people to stop talking. Homer Barron's going to silence them—and we're going to clear an honest profit off him too."

~

Not a day went by that month without Emily finding a way to parade around central Jefferson in the company of Homer Barron. You'd see them riding on Sunday afternoons, the Yankee nearly flaying the flesh off his team. You'd meet them promenading along the more fashionable streets, past the half-finished war monument and the offices of the Sentinel & Clarion, Barron's sinewy arm tucked around Emily's podgy waist. One morning, Emily sent me to the jeweler's to retrieve a monogramed toilet set; two days later, I carried home three gentleman's suits and a stack of linen undergarments from the tailor's. And each evening at six o'clock, the burly northerner deposited Emily outside her front gate and dashed off to spend his night carding and carousing with the boys at the Elks Club. "Tedious bore," complained Emily, peeling off her suede riding gloves. "But he's got money stashed away, all right." On another night, she held her face in her hands and said, "Insufferable, really. He'd better be richer than a Jew."

Then Indian summer came, and the sidewalks were all done paved, and word went about that the Baptist minister's wife had penned a letter to those dowdy Grierson cousins in Alabama, decrying Emily's traffic with Homer Barron. Unseemly, she called it. "Meddlesome crone," griped Emily. "Alas, there's no putting off the business any longer." But the business had to be put off another two weeks, because both Alabama cousins showed up, aunt and niece, setting the household at sixes and sevens, and letting half the civilized world know they wouldn't receive a call from the Yankee foreman, nor would Emily, while they slept under her roof. The pair had a chance of staying on forever too, I believe, if Emily hadn't suggested—ever so polite—that her kinfolk might sleep more comfortable at the hotel on Forrest Street. Now did that send the two meatless birds packing in a huff! "Ninnies," said Emily, dismissing her relations forever.

And the very next afternoon, I found myself eavesdropping from the scullery. "I want you close at hand," insisted Emily, "should I need assistance." I'd hardly hidden myself among the tablecloths and the Turkish towels when Homer Barron's heels tracked into the foyer.

"Where's the houseboy?" he called. "Time for a bourbon."

"Tobe is off for the afternoon," said Emily. "I'll fix you a drink."

"What is with you people? You fight a darn war to keep your chattel and now you treat them like royalty...."

Emily did not reply directly. I heard the clinking of crystal on the sideboard, then the sound of Homer Baron's torso settling into the upholstery. Inside the scullery, the air hung hot and smelled vaguely of lavender.

"So I've been intending to speak with you," said Emily, "about a business mater."

A long pause followed. Nothing was visible through the keyhole of the scullery, except darkness.

"What sort of business would this be?" asked Homer Barron.

"The business of matrimony," replied Emily

"Like I've told you before, I'm not a marrying man," said Homer Barron. "I've made no secret about that and I won't be railroaded into anything."

"Because you prefer the company of men," suggested Emily.

"If you phrase it that way. Well, yes. I do." I could hear Homer Barron's weight shifting, his boots coming down off the hassock. "Are you insinuating something?"

"Not insinuating. Just saying."

"And what precisely are you just saying?"

"I'm saying that I've seen where your eyes go."

"Have you now?"

"I have. And no good comes from folks talking," said Emily. "So what I'm proposing is that I am in need of a husband—a husband who can keep folks from gossiping and will pay off my taxes in Jefferson—and you're in need of a wife who won't give two slaps if your eyes wander after the delivery lad from the saddler's. Or more than your eyes."

"I fear you're mistaken," said Homer Barron.

"Oh, am I? In that case, I'm sorry I mentioned the matter. Truly," said Emily. "May I top off your bourbon?"

So Emily poured Homer Barron a second bourbon, and then a third, and he filled the void between them with a bawdy tale about an Irish prostitute, thoroughly unsuited for the ears of a lady, and he hammered home the point by slapping his breeches. "Which leads me to my own matter of business," said Homer Barron. "I'll be moving on. Soon as I get my accounts settled. I'm taking my outfit down to Biloxi."

"We'll be sorry to see you go," replied Emily. "Will you be laying sidewalks in Biloxi?"

"That's the business I was intending to speak with you about," he said. "What I'm hoping to do is start a cannery. Shrimp. Sardines. Good investment, if you don't mind my saying, for a woman like yourself. Considerable potential."

So them two were carved from the same timber after all. Now I fathomed why the Yankee foreman had been dallying with Emily; he was set to swindle her. Nobody done told him all the Grierson money had long gone the way of all flesh.

I heard Emily's slippers cross the walnut floor, a heavy, uneven patter like the barrage of a violent rainstorm. "Is that soooo?" she cried—and then came two dull thumps, the louder as Homer Barron's head cracked against the parquet.

First I saw the Yankee, blood trickling from his temple. And then I caught sight of Emily, both fists gripping the handle of the fire iron.

"Help me tie him up. Quickly," she instructed. She'd stashed a loop of cord behind the china hutch, and it was only a few minutes before we had Homer Barron tightly bound at the wrists and ankles, his mouth stuffed with oil rags.

"Take him into Papa's chamber, will you?"

I did as I was told, heaving the trussed Yankee onto the duvet and locking the door behind me from the outside. Then I set about tidying the parlor: emptying the ashes from the cuspidor, scrubbing bourbon out of the damask.

"Be careful with that," warned Emily. "There's arsenic in it."

I glanced up at her from my knees, half disbelieving her rage.

"Arsenic," she repeated. "That's what he earned for wasting my time." She stashed the wrought-iron poker back in the stand. "Don't you get any ideas about running off to Biloxi, Tobe—or anywhere else."

~

The groans lasted about two days, deep and woeful; then we didn't hear another peep from Homer Barron. "Now's a good time to sail to France, don't you think?" I hinted, reflecting upon my own valuation of my hide—but Emily would have none of it.

"No reason to go anywhere," she said. "People in France talk exactly like people here, only in a different language."

I hadn't given much thought to people in France speaking French, until that moment. And if I hadn't figured out how I'd buy food from folks who didn't speak English, or risk starving to death, there were probably other things I hadn't paid heed to neither. So I kept my own counsel on the subject, and went about the cooking and the gardening, and one morning I looked at myself in the drawing room window and saw I'd become one of those ancient, stooped Negroes, like the butlers that done served Master Jonas's father and grandfather. Emily was old too, squat as a tub, her hair as gray as the fire irons in the parlor. That was about when the first fire engines appeared in Jefferson, and I told Emily, thinking she might want a glimpse through the jalousies, but she spit into a napkin. "I'd rather the whole town burned to cinders," she said. And later she showed me the growth in her neck, but forbid me from sending for the doctor.

"What are you going to do when I'm dead?" asked Emily.

That was a darn good question, I thought. But she meant it other than I did. Yet that very afternoon we came up with our plan—for it's hard to say whether it was her idea first, or mine, there being nearly no daylight between us by then; so she clipped a strand of hair and gave it to me for safekeeping. "Might as well thumb my nose at them one final time," she said, smiling bitterly and pushing her soup bowl from her place setting. And when I found myself strolling to the grocer's at midweek, whistling and stepping off the sidewalk for the young white couples, that very sidewalk that Homer Barron had sacrificed so much for, it struck me that, if I didn't love Emily Grierson, and I don't reckon I did, then at least I was mighty darn fond of her. But I was mighty fond of myself as well, so I filled up Master Jonas's Gladstone with a few silver dollars—what remained of her earnings from long-abandoned china paining lessons—and the tin of arsenic. I was wise to prepare too: Three weeks later, Emily Grierson picked up a touch of the pleurisy and climbed the ladder to Heavenly Glory.

I did as we'd planned: unsealed the door of Master Jonas's chamber, cautious not to disturb the dust, and with a camphor-soaked cloth over my nose, I patted a woman's form into the bedding. Then came a strand of Emily's iron-gray hair. Nothing ever looked so natural. Or unnatural. But I'm sure some of those buzzards are already taking comfort in that hair: at least, they're whispering, Miss Emily was sleeping alongside a Yankee corpse, which ain't regular, but better than sharing a bed with a Negro. When I reach Paris, Lord willing, I'll write those bastards in Jefferson a letter with the truth.

Mason Boyles

Erosion

We found him like that. What I mean is, he was dead.

This was on the beach, in the middle of the sand dunes where we weren't supposed to be walking, but my wife and I were walking there anyway. And here was this corpse.

"Jesus!" Mary said. She was a military brat. It took a lot for her to appeal to any authority higher than herself.

"He's dead," I said.

"It's dead," Mary said. She was right.

I looked at him, half-burrowed under a blanket and a pile of grocery bags. "Was he homeless?"

"Must have been."

"Should we call someone?"

"No," Mary said. "We really shouldn't."

Then she wrapped her hands around my neck and kissed me. I still wasn't used to the slick feel of her wedding band against my skin; this was our honeymoon, after all, and we were only two days married.

The part of the Outer Banks we stayed on that November was skeletal. The pastel beach houses were sparse and empty; everything had already closed down for the winter. This was how we'd wanted it—an entire town to ourselves, sand and water and air for us to grow into each other.

But here was this dead man tucked against the dunes.

For the rest of our time there we didn't talk about it. We stayed on the beach to the north of the house Mary's parents had rented for us, smoked cigars naked on the porch and tried to plunge into an ocean so cold it was sticky.

We would mention him later, but only peripherally. It became a kind of prayer that we recited to each other.

"Remember him? Like that?"

We only ever said 'like that' because both of us had been there and we didn't need to try to describe it. After a while we stopped even saying 'like that', and we would just give each other a certain look across the kitchenette or a touch on the couch, and that would be enough for us to know: now. *Remember it.*

The first time we talked about it was after the divorce.

Our house was barren—me leaving, Mary selling—and we stood in the middle of the living room with the last of our boxes, sharing one more six pack of Fat Tire. There was a feeling of ending but also of opening. The walls were down. Now we could breathe.

"So the dead guy," Mary said. She was sitting cross-legged on the carpet where the coffee table used to be. I had stayed standing.

"Yeah," I said. A valve cranked loose somewhere deep in my grey matter; I was relieved but I wasn't surprised. "Do you remember how blue he was?"

"Like a bus sign." She smiled at that like she meant it as a joke.

Maybe she had—sometimes it was hard for me to remember how much I used to know about her. Eighteen years of marriage and I had more questions leaving than I did when we started.

"It's weird," she said, "how many times I've thought about it since then."

I nodded. "Every day."

"Every day."

My wife—my ex wife—sat down her beer. Mary. Forty-two and still saline, she had a kind of rippling prettiness that made you think you were seeing her through water. Now I'd started to wonder whether I was drowning.

"I have dreams about him," she said.

———

After I'd finished the beers I drove down Carolina Beach Road slower than I should have, slower than I wanted to, even. A Dominican couple had just closed on the house—I didn't have a reason to go back there anymore.

There were only a few things that scared me; starting over was one of them.

Mary and I had spent the last five years growing apart together. Neither of us wanted to be the one to admit that it wasn't working, I think, so she did the brave thing and gave me a reason to leave her: an affair with her quiverig boss at the real estate company. She did that for me, and even when I filed for separation at the county clerk's office I knew she'd only made me love her more. Maybe it was just a different kind of love.

Now—alone in my empty rental house, waiting for the end of Sunday—I had to decide what I was supposed to do. I thought I might build a shed in the backyard, ask the landlord for permission. I could start drawing. Take salsa lessons. But all of that seemed forced. Those were distractions, not desires. What did I need? What did I want?

I looked out the window and thought about Mary on the beach, the sand and the wind trickling around us, the things we'd thought we shouldn't say.

I wanted to drive to Cape Hatteras and find out about the dead man.

———

Hatteras was a stretched out sand dune. The trees were stretched out shrubs. The people—the few folks who lived here year round—stretched out their hopes for fall, for spring and for the first part of summer before the tourists and mosquitos.

There was a Ramada Inn on the south side of Buxton. I checked in for two nights and sat on the edge of the bed while I called my wife.

"I'm in Buxton," I said.

"Why?"

"I need to find out about that dead man."

She sighed—behind the phone filter it sounded more like a curse. "Charlie. Is this about what I told you yesterday? I was drunk. It wasn't important."

I laid back on the bedspread. The ceiling was painted with a kind of distressed pattern, I guess so you wouldn't notice mildew stains. Looking at it sent anchors through the backs of my eyes.

"No," I said. "This is about me."

———

When my wife and I bought a house together we hadn't known what we were looking for. This was before she got her real estate license, back when she was in art school and the only things that made sense to us were Cheers and the Sudoku puzzles we kept on our bedside tables. We'd go to open houses and listen to realtors talk about floor plans or down payments, trying to look like we understood.

What my wife wanted most were spare bedrooms. She was twenty-six then; she still thought she wanted to have kids. We never talked about it, but I could tell by the way she chewed on her thumbnail every time we found out one of my old college friends was going to be a dad, like any child that wasn't hers put her farther away from getting pregnant. I should have brought it up myself but I was afraid to ask her. I didn't even know what I wanted yet.

The thing that finally convinced us to buy our house—her house, now, but the one where we'd spent sixteen years together before that—was stupid. It was the kind of idea that might seem logical in a dream, when you weren't thinking linearly, but as soon as you woke up you could see all the ruts in the train tracks.

We'd decided to marry each other in a dream, I think, because now when I look back those wedding rings made no more sense than the baby or the dead man that we never talked about.

We bought that house because of a skylight.

It was in the master bedroom, right where you'd be looking if you laid flat on your back in the middle of our king sized—this was under the assumption that you put the king sized up against the far wall where my wife wanted it, but for me that had been less assumption than fact.

"I like it," my wife said. "We can stargaze."

We'd been on the market for three months by then; I was tired, whittled all the way down to the marrow.

To my wife I said, "Sure, yes, okay, very good."

To the realtor I said, "How much?"

A month later we were lining up the king sized under the skylight. Pretty soon after that I started sleeping on my stomach.

————

Monday morning it was raining. I woke up at nine and laid there, not moving, trying to imagine what it would be like to die. I pictured a spiral, a set of concentric circles dropping down toward the south side of infinity. A pairing down of motion. A stillness of thought. Meditation in theory, not in practice.

When I couldn't make my heart beat any slower I rolled out of bed and checked the clock: 9:03. Death got boring pretty quick, I guess.

I went to the library first. There would be old newspapers, I assumed, some kind of archives. The woman at the counter pointed through a door that looked like an emergency exit. "Record room. Check the file cabinets."

The cabinets sprouted all the way up to the ceiling. They looked like someone got paid to polish them regularly. I walked down to the end of the wall. I walked back to the other end. I walked down again, then back, then stopped somewhere close to the middle. I still had no idea what I was supposed to be looking for.

I stood there looking at my reflection in the front of the cabinets until I felt stupid. A librarian stuck her head through the door. She wanted to know if I needed help.

"No," I said. "I was about to leave."

Outside of the library there was a tent full of Baptists. They were handing out cookies and scones, selling them for some charity I didn't recognize. There were pictures of smiling African children hanging up in the tent. I guess those kids needed the money more than they needed the baked goods.

"Want a muffin?" A lady said.

"No thanks," I said.

"But they're for charity. What about the children?"

I stopped at the curb and so did she. The edge of the asphalt must have been some kind of invisible barrier. "I never had any," I said.

My wife had never gone to church, so I didn't go either.

————

Back at the hotel it was still raining. It felt like rain might be all there was to this place, water and sand and wind all tugged down by gravity. The idea of going to the library seemed ridiculous, driving up here to look at a row of file cabinets—and I didn't know where else to look. I didn't know anything.

The hotel lobby was full of men in business suits. They were talking about portfolios and waiting for the elevator; I took the stairs instead, got to my room and turned on the TV.

My wife would be at work by now, in her office or in her car on the way to a house she was selling. If she was in the car she would be listening to a book on tape, a Tom Clancy novel. If she was in the office she would be doing Sudoku. Her boss would be leaning on the edge of her table trying to flirt with her. Sometimes it scared me how beautiful she still was—it was the kind of thing that could scare anyone.

I picked up the phone. I was starting to get an idea of what I was doing.

"Hello?" My wife said.

"Hey," I said. "It's me."

"Are you still in Buxton?"

"Yeah," I said. "Still here." Someone was yelling in the hallway. Not words—not syllables, even—just sound.

My wife breathed gut-deep; this must not have been a good time. "Did you find anything?"

"There were scones," I said. "And church people. But no, not really."

"Church people?"

"Outside the library."

"Oh," she said, and she made that one word a sentence.

Silence, five seconds. I needed to ask her things. "Have the people signed the deed yet?"

"Yep," she said. "Just this morning."

"So that's it?"

"It's done."

I knew she was right but I couldn't feel it. I had to keep pressing. "You never told me where you were living."

"Stuart—I have to go."

"I wish you hadn't sold our house."

"Bye," she said. The buzz of an empty line quivered through my phone. It didn't mean anything, I told myself. It was just sound.

———

On Wednesday I checked out of the hotel.

"How was your stay?" The clerk at the front desk asked me.

"I'm not sure," I said. I sounded like an asshole but I was just being honest.

It had dropped below fifty overnight. I had to smear my hands over the windshield to clear away the condensation. My wife had chosen this car for me because it was fuel efficient. She was my ex wife now, but I still had this car.

I turned up the heater until my fingers were sweating. There was one more thing I had to do.

I drove to the last beach access with a cigarette and the windows down. Before I left Buxton I'd stopped at an Exxon for a pack of Marlboros; I hadn't smoked since I asked my ex wife to marry me.

The road split south down the beach, dark and smooth and basically straight even though the coastline was puckered with divots. Purple storm clouds lumped together over the ocean. Rain was coming.

I stopped when the road did. This was the edge of the island, the channel where the waterway slopped into the ocean. It was two miles past the place where we had found the dead man.

I took off my shoes. I started walking.

This beach ran north for fifty miles. I looked and looked for the other end but it was tucked somewhere behind the horizon line. Up there the dunes and the tideline and the ocean all converged, twisting together into something impossible. I'd heard that the earth was actually an oval; to me it looked triangular.

I didn't notice the rain until my shirt was stuck to my chest, until my feet fit into the sand a little easier. Here was a flat topped sand dune. I had no way of knowing if this was really the spot where we had found him, but I told myself that it was. I got on my hands and my knees and I crawled to the crook where the dune met the beach. The dead man had been lying on his side. I lay on my side. The dead man's eyes were open. I kept my eyes open, too, and I waited and waited to feel something.

The rain fell. The wind trickled grains of sand across my face. Nothing was happening.

I didn't call my ex wife.

The 2015 Lorian Hemingway Short Story Competition Winner

Lizzy Welby

The Breakers

'Joseph said she was the first one he found from the wreck. He went out to check his lobster pots and there she was.'

I see her. *Face down in the water, shoulders heaving in the swell as if trying to lift herself up.*

There are black-tipped gulls dipping fast in low arcs across the water today. Crisscrossing close but never touching. Scraps of cloud hang under the chalky backbone of a mackerel sky. The wind is stilled and waiting; hibernating in the wrong season. Last night the sea was black silk beyond the breakers. We heard nothing but her distant whispers as she rolled over and over, spilling out onto the rocks below the lighthouse at *Créac'h.*

'Oh Gaël, how did he get her?'

'With his *pech*, Corrine. He lost his grip as he hauled her into the boat and the hook got caught in her mouth.'

The *Pierres Vertes* have ensnared another ship, gouged grooves across her hull. The Fromveur runs deep and fast between Ouessant and Molène. Swift, churning currents. *I see frantic souls piercing the oily, sheeted surface of the sea. I see others sucked down with a dead weight of metal that twists their bones into new shapes.* A woman has drifted to Ouessant, long hair fanning out around her as she glides quietly through the night. Her course collided with Joseph at first light. She is the first. There will be others; corpses waiting for us all along our coastline.

'Help me get her inside, Corinne. I've got to go back with Yann to look for others.'

The sea is already brining bodies for the host of fish that will follow in the wreck's wake.

The **muscles** on my husband's arms stand out like rigging as he reaches down to our vegetable cart where this woman lays. She is flattened and wet. Gaël lifts up her arms at the wrists and pulls. White fingers brush the inside of my husband's forearms. He twists around to haul this dead weight onto his back. I put my palm in the middle of his spine to steady him. He jigs forward, bending his knees to balance the weight and this slight movement tilts her backwards. I cup the back of her head with both hands and lay it on his shoulder. Matted tendrils shroud his face from me. He takes her across the threshold of our home, along the passage and lays her gently down on my kitchen table. I try not to look at the tear that pulls the corner of her mouth up into a crooked smile. Spots of blue and green flicker on her pale skin from sunlight caught in the painted lead spheres that hang suspended from the ceiling. There are nine of them. One for each year that Gaël has been at sea. Bright keepsakes for our black days.

'I'll be back soon. I'm going to pick up Yann on the way.'

My husband moves across the window frame hatted and serious to join the men rowrowing their little dories before the tide rolls the corpses to the rocks where the seaweed will hold them. Some will be floating face down, dresses billowing, frockcoats flapping as though flying above the bright blue waters, watching fishermen plucking dead things below. Some will lie snagged on the shoreline, skin torn on the broken teeth of the rocks.

Hélène replaces Gaël in my window frame. Her shadow moves across the body of this woman. Hélène is dressed in her church best. Hair tucked under a white lace *coiffe*. I set the water to boil. There are rituals to be observed once again. The dead need attention. I hear my friend lift the latch and step down onto the earthen floor of my home. A soft hiss of the sea flows into my house for a moment until pushed back by the closing door. She moves quietly along the passage.

'Yann said the ship sank last night.'

'Oh Hélène, does anyone know how it happened?'

'He says they were off course. The ship was heading for England and should have rounded at Ouessant but they turned north too early. Yann says the Captain must have mistaken Molène for Ouessant.'

'Was anyone pulled out alive?'

'One. He floated all night on three life belts he'd tied together. He was in bad shape when they picked him up.'

'Where is he now?'

'In Lampaul, at the *Mairie* with Monsieur Malgorn. Charles Marquardt is his name. He speaks French and said that there was a dance going on when the steamer hit the reef. It was their last night on board. There was no time to do anything. The ship went down in a few minutes.'

I hear voices shouting in a foreign language, twisting and turning in terror then slowly extinguished as the night wears out. Cold waters claim them, quietly, one by one.

'How many were lost?'

'I'm not sure. A hundred at least, Yann thinks, maybe more. *War ma fé, heman zo eun Anko drouk.* It's a nasty *Ankou*. He'll have more than enough souls to fill his barrow from this wreck.'

'Monsieur Malgorn told Gaël that the ones they found will be buried here on Ouessant. There is only enough wood to make coffins for the women and children. The men will be buried in sailcloth.'

In our cemetery at Lampaul there is a mausoleum, as small as a doll's house. For the men whose bodies are lost to sea we have a ritual, the *Pröella*. A little wax cross stands in for the corpse. It is placed up on top of all the other crosses that are stacked up in the *Pröella* tomb and mourned as if it were a man sealed into the earth. More crosses will be added after this wreck. But for now we turn our attention to the drowned woman lying between us. The space is cramped with the three of us. Breton houses are like boats. Everything has its place and is stowed away. The doors to the bed boxes are fastened open for the day and I feel Gaël's presence in each piece of furniture he has made for us from the driftwood that washes up on shore from wrecks.

'Help me get her jacket off, Hélène. We've got to get her ready for the priest.'

I pour hot water into my flowered bowl. The water rushes in waves that spill over the edge before spiraling back on themselves to lap gently at the sides. The little painted *bonhomme* struggles beneath the ripples for a moment before lying still at the bottom. Hélène tucks back the sleeves on her shirt. Her spidery fingers pleating neat folds over and over, exposing skin almost as white as the woman lying between us. A black lace jacket over sea-blue silk is all this woman is wearing. One shoe is buttoned. One shoe is lost.

I hear panicky shouts. No time for a coat. No time for a lifebelt. No time to button both shoes. Rush-rushing against a tilting deck. Hands grip a guardrail. Sliding. Toppling. Arcing wide across a steel shadow. Ribbons of time unravel from the tips of your fingers, spindling skyward. Then ancient stars are doused in icy darkness.

This woman stiffly resists my touch. I lift her at the shoulders and her head snaps to one side. Clear seawater trickles from the dark shell of her mouth, running in rivulets through her broken lips. The sea contracts, once, twice, three times then opens. Spiralling you downwards. Feet first. Folding you into a body full of destruction. Silvery bubbles of life tendril around one arrowed arm then dart away. Lives tear. A wife; a life's pivot spinning away from you. Fine filaments of green weed swirl through broken lips before being swept away in streams that race across her cheek. The clear liquid gives way to a sticky black tar that pools around the gash.

'Take this', says Hélène handing me a white cloth. 'It's come up from the lungs.'

'Help me with move her up, Hélène. She needs to be washed.'

This woman is heavy and moves with no willed direction, like a doll. The cloth in my hand is streaked black. I peel strands of hair from her forehead, long coppery hair uncurled from the pin that has dredged up lopsided in its tangles. It crackles with dried salt that stings my hands. Her skin is slippery and white save for the inky stain on her cheek.

Who did you fight for as you tore through the sea's silk skeins? What thoughts were yours as you emerged from a green silence into the clamour of life beating the water black? Les bras de mer elongate and embrace you. Lips are thumbed open and cold fingertips reach down to hook out the one white breath you kept for the end.

Her skin begins to mottle as we set to work. Taking a cloth, Hélène smooths hot water over her body in long swift strokes and I soap her hair. Sand grits under my hand and flecks of seaweed get caught in the cloth.

'Do you think there is a husband in another house? Or maybe a child? Yann told me they'd taken a little girl from the wreck.'

'I don't know, Hélène. Perhaps.'

These are questions for another time. For now, I cover her with a white sheet that will stand in for a shroud. Today is a day filled with chores for the living. No time to think about other bodies lying under lamplights all over our island.

Our home is to be a chapel for the time that this woman stays with us. My kitchen disappears behind the white linen sheets we pin over cracked plaster and sooty smudges. Together we lay my mother's silver candlesticks, two at her head and two and her feet then Hélène pins ribbons to small sprays of boxwood that will serve as a headdress. We place faded paper flowers in a pile at her feet ready to pin to her clothes when we dress her. I roll sprigs of flowering boxwood between my fingers and place them in porcelain dishes at the foot of my table. The scent intensifies with the heat of the fire, the other smell settles down beneath. Hélène lights four pale candles and leaves me to wait for the priest. *The sea whispers names over and over, names of the drowned. Stilled lives lying waked all over our island.*

*****

'Pennec has offered to lay out all the bodies before burial. Can you make a coffin, Gaël?'

'Of course. I'll get Yann to help me, *Abbé*.'

'Over 240 souls drowned in one night. The ones brought here will be buried on Friday. Can you make it by then?'

'Of course, *Abbé*. I'll get to work tomorrow. We'll carve and paint it by Friday. Where are the bodies going?'

'To the lifeboat house in *Porsguen*. The women are preparing it tomorrow. Can you help Corinne?'

'Yes, *Abbé*. I'll go with Hélène in the morning.'

'Goodnight Gaël. Goodnight Corinne.'

'Goodnight *Abbé.*'

Gaël moves into the light and leaves a rectangle of darkness as he watches Hervé, and Jean-Luc take the sheeted woman and load her into the cart. I can hear the jangle of bells on harnesses as the horses stamp the black night, restless to be moving. The sea swishes. The wind swirls the sound all around my home. The woman is gone. The fire is lit and I begin to take down the linens from my kitchen. Slowly, racks of china are brought back into view. Pardons from St Michael and St Paul emerge from behind their white covers. Tomorrow bread will prove in the trough under my table. Soft breath murmurs into the strands that have escaped my coiffe. Fingertips smooth my shoulders. I tilt my head to my shoulder and Gaël's breath eddies in the hollows. My husband leans me into his front and holds me fast for a moment. I feel his weight, hands crossed over my belly, pulling me close to seal the gaps.

The sheets on our marriage bed are as white marble as he lays me down. He presses my hand to his heart and I feel its steady beats. Outside the wind has risen. Blowing in from the west, bringing boiling clouds and black rain.

The wind carries away all things. Ribbons and scraps. Voices and memory. Mariners. The dust of you. Billowing. Circling. Blown headlong down passages, forced between cracks in the window frames, shoved through gaps in the door then flung high into the night air. Rushing upwards. Colliding in a thousand thin columns then smashed back against the coastal rocks. The wind scoops up fistfuls of you and hurls them at the light-house. Créac'h's white light slice ignites the specks again and again. Fiery fragments fade over the waves. Red embers of memory.

My husband is carved out of the leaden air, unmoving. In this room, with the memory of his hands in every piece of furniture he has made for me, he is here and I feel the sharp splinters of life. His body ripples and pulses with longing. Life wisps and flickers within this room gusting over the imprint left by a cold woman on our bed sheets. His arms reach for me. As he turns me over, I see his body lit from beneath with a blood-red light of the dying fire. I feel life moving deep inside me in currents that drift and run. All over Gaël's body sweat prickles, cold and fresh like the tidal mouth of the river. Grey eyes are fixed wide on nothing. La petite morte. Gaël's heart calms. And this is life.

The Widows of Ouessant spin away from me, their bodies encased within their black cloaks, shattering one after the other on the breakers. Each lamed by life, each rigged and brigged, each with an eye trained on the horizon for a mariner that will never come home. Each a living reminder of the cost of our island life.

For a long time I listen to the sound of Gaël's breathing that pitches higher than the wind and the creaking sea.

*****

I smell the sweet peas before Hélène and I reach the front of the lifeboat house. Sweet peas in season. Sweet peas to decorate the dead house. The old wooden doors are slatted open, facing the water, and I feel the murmur of activity. It moves in time with the waves that struggle to gain purchase on the pebbles.

A group of gulls are sitting in the sea close to the jaggy barbed rocks that sit in the middle of the Bay of *Penn ar Roc'h*. Many more are clustered on the leeward side of the rocks. A solitary gull is circling the waves, swooping into the water, tearing at the skin of the sea, flicking its head this way and that before pitching back into the sky, black-tipped wings flapping wildly as though the sea might grab it back down. I hear its rasping caw fade as it flies beyond the rocks.

My dear Hélène takes my hand and pulls me up to stand in front of the doors. I can feel her cold hand through my shirtsleeve. It is steering me. The smell of sweet peas is overwhelming. I am submerged. I look up and see the coffin that my husband has made standing upright at the end of the room. In the middle Gaël has carved a posy of nasturtiums protected by their shield-shaped leaves. A wooden corsage for Maggie McGee. There are bodies everywhere. Figures standing, moving around, figures lying on the floor in neat rows as if sleeping, figures kneeling between the two. I can see the woman with the black crack that streaks across the side of her face. Maggie McGee.

Maggie McGee, dressed in your fêted best, booted and bolted into the leaking earth. Pale burrowing creatures, darting through the soil to reach you. Resistance. Silently settling down to wait for the white wood to fail. A rotten spray of nasturtiums no defence.

The sweet pea scent plugs my nose. I am drowning. I see Hélène walking toward me, sleeves rolled up, wiping her hands on a white apron, faster now, before darkness falls over everything.

*****

Yann and Felix take their places on the stage to mourn the dead in song at the *FestNoz*. Both men have removed their stiff black jackets and round rib-boned hats. White shirts sag like empty sails. Yann begins it. The skeleton of the Gavotte. Calling to Felix. Waiting for a response. The *bombarde* is always played with the *binioù kozh*. Woodwind and Bagpipe. Always together. Yann plays the bombarde as if the world is ending; all his strength focused on one point, on two thin reeds at the lip of his mouthpiece.

Gaël moves toward the black and white eddying shreds that are beginning to swell then halts. In my mind's eye, I see mariners crawling like insects over the body of a ship. Waking her in her winter quarters. White fingertips spidering over running rigging, feeling for the smooth give of the cordage. I see Gaël with one hand on the mizzenmast and the other on Yann, swaying in time to the sea's own rhythm while a wind-blown island becomes a needle point on a widening horizon. My boots have grown green roots. Sprouting slantwise they scrabble across a black floor. Unable to penetrate the iron earth, I am snagged in the wash of music. The strains of Yann's *Gavotte* reeling me toward my husband. I want no part of this dance. I want no lasts. But I am propelled forward.

Arms aloft, fingertips entwined with our neighbours, Gaël and I are pulled sideways into the rhythm. Bodies stack up, bumping together, as we move faster and faster in a circled line around the dance floor. Yann spins out the dance, accelerating then slowing, accelerating then slowing on a whim, pulling Felix along in the game. I pick out Hélène in the monochrome smudge, breathless and laughing. Charles Marquardt is caught up in the line. Unsteady on his feet, unsure of the steps, he is held firm by two black-*coiffed* widows, who guide him through the dance. Here at this *Fest-Noz* the memory of blue bloated bodies is crushed beneath our black boots. A chain of dancers, side-by-side, sharing the timbre of a fleeting *jouissance*. On and on and on and on. Endless repetitive steps
.

Pleated time. Clamping a wreck in the dark. Booted feet whirling round and round. Stamping out life in duple time. Flushed cheeks. Damp breasts. Spinning. Twirling. Eyes alight and flashing. Heads back. Breathless. Threads of time stretch and sag between fingertips. Dead steps we dance. Unraveling our spools of time.

Yann won't stop. Eight shattering notes are hammered onto the trailing strains of the *Gavotte*. The old song. *Kan An Alarc'h*. One voice answers. Joseph Berthele. His voice rings through a quieting crowd. *Kan An Alarc'h*. A song for armies. A song for marching. A song for leave-taking. Voices join the swelling sound. Mariners merging. Words gutter. Englishmen are stilled by a chant in Breton that is stronger than any words spoken by a priest. Strong enough to truly wake the dead. And now they come, as I always knew they would. An unbroken line of drowned sailors marching into the throng, some with splintered Pröella crosses pressed close to their chests, some with faded paper flowers pinned tight to their shirts. Mariners mourned into life.

'Dinn, dinn, daoñ d'an emgann ez an! Dinn, dinn, daoñ to the fight we go!'

Over and over and over and over. Roaring as one in song. An endless repetitive refrain. Gaël moves toward the stage and something deep within my body judders. *A flicker, a pulse, a ghostfish. But hardly. Setting sail from a wreck in the dark. A raggy thrumming thing eddies through a dark red pool, drinking all the water. Swelling. Slowing. Stretched. Coffined. Caught upside down in a sticky caul.* My husband, my Gaël, is pulled across the gap that has opened up between Ouessantine women and their sea-bound husbands, swaying in time to the sea's own rhythm. Our language rises from the past, carrying them all, craving and cut loose, out over the breakers, *toward brittle boats in the frozen north, toward heaving nets and churning storms, toward the end,* spiraled inside the terrible wind that is rising in this room. Charles Marquardt, the only survivor, stands stock still amongst a host of straight-backed Ouessantines, all turned toward our mariners, *déjà dans les bras de la mer traîtresse,* singing through the storm that rages across time. *Dinn, dinn, daoñ d'an emgann ez an!* Dinn, dinn, daoñ to the fight we go!

Bobbie Ann Mason

The Belly Dancer And The Flamenco Guitarist

Since she hurt her hand lifting weights and could manicure only one hand, she had become restless, bored with belly dancing at the Mute Flamingo Supper Club. She wanted to do something more exotic--like the splashy sambas of Carmen Miranda, who wiggled her bare midriff in ecstasy while balancing a fruit display on her head.

Why not flamenco dancing? She longed to dance with the flamenco guitarist who played the last slot of the evening.

"Swedish eyes," the dreamy flamenco guitarist had said to her yesterday in passing.

He wouldn't explain.

He sat on a stool and made love to his guitar, patting it and ruffling it and then making it scream and thrill. He banged the box with his fretless hand, then strummed violently, eyes closed, quieter and quieter, then louder and louder, softer and softer--as if he were going to break into "Twist and Shout" with the Isley Brothers--but then erupting in a frenzy of strumming. He rocked back and forth, his mouth agape, lost in his own reverie, like someone having eventful sex.

Then rising toward the crescendo, he played the box like bongos. His radical, violent, chaotic strumming sent a torrent of flame through her belly. Her belly was her energy center, according to tai chi, which she had been lax about lately, even though she liked the idea of it and it helped with her belly toning.

She stayed late in the evenings, keeping an eye on the flamenco guitarist. His toupee resembled dyed feathers.

"I have a homeopathic treatment for your injured hand," he offered when she lingered after his performance at the Mute Flamingo to talk with him. "It is at my home. Home--homeopathic. Get it? You will need to come to my home."

"Can I see your etchings too?"

He didn't smile. You can never tell what trite jokes people don't know, she thought.

The homeopathic flamenco guitarist in the jumpy toupee led her to his car. She moved on cat feet. She definitely needed her belly rubbed. He had promised to massage her hand at least. She followed, skidding a little on the flagstones, feeling flimsy and foolish. With her belly relaxed, she felt receptive, vulnerable. Although she wanted to have a natural high with him, she hoped they wouldn't be whiffing something. Her nose was stopped up and the antihistamine she had taken was wearing off.

Swedish eyes, she thought with pleasure. She made a mental list of Swedish actresses.

Greta Garbo in "Queen Christina."

Ingrid Bergman. Anita Ekberg.

She couldn't remember anything about their eyes.

His house was modest. He sat her down on a love seat and offered her a chai tea with infusion of stevia leaf and blackberry leaf. He had a sweet face. At the supper club the waiters had a bad opinion of him because he played sissy, foreign guitar. The head waiter was ruthless, unjustly withholding salutations and lifting his eyes superciliously.

From his pantry the flamenco guitarist chose a bottle of grape-seed oil, something she had on her own shelf in her tiny studio apartment, but he had probably paid a premium for it from some quack homeopath.

"You must warm the fingers," he said. "I warm my fingers to keep them flexible."

He massaged her hand with a solvent to cut grease.

"What grease?"

He didn't answer. Then he said, "We purify the hand."

"You should know about hands. Playing the guitar."

"The hand is a precious instrument. I take exquisite care of my hands."

"Watching you play, I'd say you are punishing your hands," she said, teasing.

"No, you have to know what you are doing. You lifted weights incorrectly and you punished your hands." He spoke reprovingly, not playfully.

Maybe the flamenco man's toupee was a medicine hat, she thought. Maybe he needed his medicine hat in order to offer his high-handed advice.

"I wish I could learn flamenco dancing," she said, continuing in playful mode.

"Then I could perform with you. I need a new challenge. Do you think I could learn flamenco? I mean, my abdomen is in good shape and it is my core, so I should be able to dance any kind of dance. Or, could we do a belly dancer and flamenco duet? That would be original." She laughed, a snicker.

He frowned. "I couldn't teach you flamenco. What I do isn't authentic."

He was wringing his hands--the first true hand wringing she had ever seen.

"But it's flamenco-ish," she said.

"It's not really flamenco with an electric guitar. Sometimes I go electric."

"But you're very good."

"I'm no Montoya." He gave a sigh, almost a sob.

She hadn't realized the homeopath medicine-man flamenco-ish guitarist was so depressed and lonely. She could imagine how he felt, wrestling with his inadequacies when he had had bigger plans for himself. She felt very sympathetic toward him because he wasn't Montoya. She could understand how he would withdraw from her. It wasn't her belly dancing. He was just disappointed in himself. He said he would take her home. Before leaving, he instructed her on how to rig up a home remedy for keeping her hands warm.

In her room, following his instructions, she filled a tube sock with rice and some aromatic herbs he had given her and knotted the end. She wrapped it in a small hand towel and heated it in the microwave. The sock smelled of lavender. She slid her injured hand inside the rolled towel and with her left hand Googled Montoya.

"I'm no Montoya," the flamenco guitarist had said.

She found Montoya on YouTube, playing something very old. He was an old guy, sitting sedately in black-and-white, but his hands were flying.

The flamenco guitarist was right. Montoya's hands, strong and agile, with long fingernails, were magnificent and speedy. His plectrum-studded strumming hand plucked the guitar with amphetamine intensity. She listened to another song, "Malagueña," that had no video with it. But once she had seen Montoya's hands, she knew them. She could feel them playing the music, the fire dancing in her belly.

Montoya's hands must have always been warm, hot with the flame of flamenco. A man born with such warm hands had a destiny.

She pressed her hot hand hard against her belly.

"I'm no Carmen Miranda," she thought

Susan Power

Indian Diva
(Mildly Autobiographical)

If you're reading this in the 22nd century—wait, let me stop right therebecause now I'm trying to imagine what reading looks like in your time. Either you're back to banging out words from a rock or you've got a device that hovers beside your ear as it reads aloud to you in the voice of a favorite actor you've preselected. Either way, if your treatment of history is at all similar to how we handle it in the strange, unraveling year of 2012, then you don't know much about what has come before. So let me tell you.

I am what we call a "mixed-blood," as most of you probably are by now. Not some being whipped up in a Lab with scientists sorting out the better parts of ancestral DNA, but the product of my parents' wild love affair that bridged great chasms of difference. When I was little I pictured my seedling born in a circus: My mother is a beautiful Native woman with thick black hair that scrapes down her back all the way to her knees, strong as an athlete, with a fine slash of nose that should be on somebody's coin. My father is elegantly handsome, a WASPy white man with blue-gray eyes and a thick mane of silver hair, rather tweedy no matter what he wears, like he's just stepped out of a lecture at Oxford. In my imaginings they are trapeze artists, wearing skin-tight leotards and leggings, my father's outfit plain, but my mother's decorated with spangles and beads. They are floating above the crowd, swinging back and forth, together and apart; a teasing courtship dance taking place in the air. Eventually they swing on opposite sides of their lofted stage and one will have to let go completely in a leap of faith that the other will catch them. It's unclear which one will do the release as they are both quite strong. The way I see it they both let go at the same time, ignoring the gasps of the crowd below, oblivious to danger. In that endless second of extended flight I am born between them – the idea of me, the reckless possibility. They clamp forearms and float slowly and safely to the net below, never breaking their gaze which is locked as tightly as their hands. And when they land the two have become three. My father assists my mother as they step out of the net because she is holding the small brown bundle of me.

I grew up in an age I like to call "When the World Was White." It wasn't merely White in terms of census numbers. Everywhere you looked – in textbooks, popular culture, leadership – white people were the norm, the standard, the valued, and the final word on everything. Television was white and the movies were white, except for a little Blaxploitation (the tragedy of Blacula!) and the lightning fists of Bruce Lee. Books and writers were white, teachers were white, doctors and nurses were white, cab drivers were white, police were definitely white, and every last president who had ever been elected was white. Natives (or "Indians" as we were called then, don't ask, long story) were so left out of the whole American scene even though this was our home continent from the beginning of time, we could get a little desperate. Any show that featured a Native character was on our watch list, even if the actor wasn't Indian at all and wore a lousy wig. It was the idea that mattered, that society was tossing a small nod in our direction as if to say, "We haven't entirely forgotten that you exist. Well. Existed." Past tense. I was raised in the past tense so I will make this story as present tense as possible and apologize for the confusion.

You can imagine our pure delight when the film *Billy Jack* hits the screens in the Seventies. Here is an Indian who can take on a whole town of bigots and whapwhap-whap their faces with his bare feet until they fall around him like broken birds. Even white people cheer him which is pretty interesting.

My mother is as fierce as Billy Jack in her way, though she keeps her shoes on. She attends demonstrations and is arrested, tries to force the government to live up to its word spelled out in treaties, which almost never happens. When cops beat on young activists, my mother beats on the cops. I watch on the sidelines because I'm too small to make a dent in the action, but I'm taking it all in for posterity and know that someday I'll strike my own kind of blow.

I love both my parents but my Dakota mother's shadow stretches across Chicago. I can hardly believe she is the little girl I've seen in the sole photograph of her as a child. She is standing in front of her family's log cabin, barefoot, wearing bib overalls and a Christopher Robin haircut that makes her look like a little boy. She scowls into the camera – sullen, hungry, dirty.

"*Unsika*," she says of herself. Pitiful. But I don't agree. Even as a reservation child growing up during the Depression, caught in the choking Dust Bowl, watching soil fly away, she looks older than her nine years. The woman is already there, behind the eyes, her gaze fierce as Medusa's. She stares down the camera lens and peers beyond the frame of scratched, wrinkled paper. There is medicine energy in her eyes as she looks into the future, into the face of her daughter who is holding the photograph in the small pinch of her fingers.

My parents named me Diva because when I was born I came out singing Patsy Cline songs, one blue number after another. I did, I'm serious.

"You didn't cry at all," Mama says. "You launched into Crazy, and the doctor dropped you -- he was so astonished. But one of those crusty old nurses who has seen everything in this life was quick enough to catch you in her thick oven mitt hands. So you didn't even hiccup, just kept on singing. I asked you to do Walking After Midnight, but you were already stubborn. You ignored my request and switched over to I Fall to Pieces instead. The medical staff kept looking at the walls and the ceiling, like a t.v. host was about to pop out with his camera and holler, 'You're on Candid Camera!' When that didn't happen the doctor said they had to put you through some tests, and they carried you off, held at arm's length like you were a dangerous load, a wriggling vial of nitroglycerin. I could hear you out there, yodeling in the halls. Your father asked me if it was some kind of Indian thing, you know, the strange singing baby episode. And I said, 'Well, Harrison, yes. We aren't like anybody else. We have secret powers from birth.' He nodded his head in a solemn way, absorbing that, and for one second I was so disgusted I nearly asked for a divorce right then and there. It's too easy to pull the myth over their eyes. Funny, he doesn't believe in spirits or God or the afterlife, but he believes in anthropological curiosities."

With a name like Diva I tend to find myself on the nasty end of trouble more often than most. By way of example let me take you back to 1970. I'm in the fourth grade at a Catholic School, yes, Catholic. Mom says this is because the Jesuits got to our reservation before the Protestants, and she hasn't yet been able to wash her hands of all that guilt. My teacher is Miss Gumm, and I've gotten to know her better than any other teacher because her hours with us are personal therapy sessions.

"I'm fragile," she tells us, though she's built like a moving van. "I have the gentle soul of an artist." We keep waiting to get some glimpse of her gentle art, but so far the only music she makes is the thwop we hear when she swats Stephen Blythe for chewing on the end of his tie.

She shows us slides of her summer vacations – trips to Hawaii and Jamaica, where she stands with legs apart and fists on her square hips, staring down the sea in a threatening way. She says men are few and far between and the good ones never travel alone to the tropics. She tells us to take notes because love trouble is the most important subject we need to know about, and she is the world's Number One Expert when it comes to Flying Solo. Stephen spits his tie out of his mouth when he hears this and asks what kind of plane she flies. She tells him to stand in the corner for that remark, though he holds out his hands in a pleading way like he doesn't understand the rules. None of us do. She makes us perform the Mexican Hat Dance around a sombrero every Friday, though none of us are Mexican. She often points to the three framed pictures that hang above her desk, saying these are the men she loves above all others. She calls them her Trinity, and a few of us bet we could get her in trouble with the nuns if we told them her trinity isn't even close to the one Monsignor worships. Miss Gumm's trinity act like monitors when we take tests, squinting down at us from on high, suspicious. Between us we figure out who they are, though she never tells us: Paul Newman, Frank Sinatra, and the president, Richard Nixon.

Miss Gumm says she's enlightened and ahead of the times, which is why she doesn't mind working in a "mixed" school. To prove her point she teaches a oneweek Social Studies unit on Indians, declaring that they weren't all as savage as John Wayne films like to show, though she assures us she likes John Wayne and it isn't his fault what words the writers put in his mouth. The first day she tells us about Southwestern tribes, shows us pictures of Navajo rugs and turquoise jewelry, cloudlike sheep herded on a mountain. The next day she focuses on tribes of the Northern Plains, my own people, the Dakota, or Sioux as she calls us, dragged into the scholastic arena in a way that makes me wince. Of course we are war-like, according to her, just look what we did to poor Custer, and we killed too many buffalo because we got greedy by the end, and my God, what we did to our women, treating them worse than servants.

"You girls are lucky," she says, and she looks straight at me. "Your quality of life will be so much better than if you were Sioux or Crow or Cheyenne."

I raise my hand but she will not call on me. She knows my background. She knows I'm not buying the party line. I keep my hand in the air all through class, using my other arm to prop it up when I become tired. I wiggle my fingers whenever she glances in my direction. Finally, just minutes before the bell rings to shuttle us on to another subject, Miss Gumm sighs and calls my name.

I tell the class that my people, the Yanktonai Dakota, are known for our great orators and counselors, and that we have some of the strongest, most fiercely political women I know.

"And my grandmother was elected chair of our tribe in the nineteen-forties," I add. "That's a very powerful position, kind of like a President."

Miss Gumm puts her hand out like a traffic cop to halt my narrative. "Hold on, hold on," she says. "That isn't what *I* read. Your women were badly treated by lazy men, and couldn't get jobs as we can. No nurses or teachers or shop ladies among them. Be glad those days are over and you're living in a civilized world."

My ears are burning now, a sure sign of rage. My face is hot as a boiled egg and my hands are shaking.

"You don't know anything about us," I hiss. "You. Don't. Know. Squat."

For a fragile woman she is quick. She covers half the classroom in what seems like a millisecond, the swift dive-bomb of a mosquito. She cracks my head with her ruler and I don't hear anything after that. My essence distills to the purely physical level. I am an angry body leaping across my desk to attach myself, Mike Tyson-like, to my teacher's pink ear. I bite like a wolf, clamp down on her perfumed flesh and jerk her head one way, then the other.

I am a wild Indian, I am thinking. I am a wild Indian and you better look out!

And I know I'm playing right into her hands, proving all her beastly bigoted points that riled me up in the first place. But I can't seem to stop myself. Miss Gumm is every stupid person who's asked me if I'm a real Indian, if we're not all dead, if we still live in tipis, if we hop in dizzy circles and call it dancing, if we're drunk all the time, lonesome for the old days when at least we still had a fighting chance. I'm at war with stupid, so I hang on to my teacher's ear until she manages to knock me out.

I left Catholic School (well, it kind of left me) but eventually squeezed myself through the education nozzle, even got good grades and ended up at Harvard. I was younger then, more patient. I moved to the Twin Cities in Minnesota to stake out my own turf, separate from my parents, where in my thirties I wrote a novel called The Professional Indian, essentially skewering every Native in the country I thought was a hypocrite or precious. The book made a bit of a splash and I spent a lot of time touring, both here and abroad. I had a business card made up with my contact information which plainly read at the top: I am NOT a professional Indian – that's just the title of my book. But it didn't do much good. I kept getting marriage proposals from men in Germany, and invitations to dance in the Norwegian woods. The French stuck me on panels of oppression where I was expected to toot my victim horn, and the Dutch wanted to photograph me nude on a bed of feathers. It was all so dreary. But then, in a small town on the Breton coast of France, I met my current boyfriend. Quanah is a young Ute dancer with long brown braids he can tuck in the band of his jeans. When he put the moves on me I carded him, he looked so young and fresh. I'm not kidding. I made him pull out his driver's license to make sure he was legal. Imagine my relief when I saw he was twenty-four to my thirty-eight. I kissed him before he had the chance to put his card away. I made him call me "Auntie."

At that time he was a member of a traveling group of dancers and singers from the Northern Plains. Quanah was their star grass dancer which I must admit is my favorite style to watch. What made the experience even sweeter was seeing the European girls swoon over Quanah with his classic Indian features and hoop earrings, his rippling grace. They tucked phone numbers in the cinch of his belt or the pockets of his jeans. They licked their sweet pink mouths and sent him air kisses he sometimes plucked but more often ducked. All of that tension and energy surrounded him like a thick hormonal cologne but I was the one, over there in the wings, who would get the spiced honey of his mouth, the best of his dancer's tricks.

Once I pry him out of Europe I convince Quanah to attend graduate school at the University of Minnesota so we can be together. He's studying History, and likes to tease me that this interest extends to his personal life. Ha ha. Much more of that and you'll get a spanking, I threaten, and he just lifts his eyebrows as if to dare me.

I wish I could end my story right here, in the middle of all my happiness, but of course there's more. I'm an Indian Diva and I never stay out of trouble for long. Each year I attend a conference on Native American Literature which is held in different locations. This year the festivities are right in my own backyard, at the Mystic Lake Casino run by a band of my people. I hear many provocative, brilliant papers, Natives on Natives, in dialogue with one another. We scrutinize each other's voices and themes, celebrate the diversity of our literary aims and angles. It's all very uplifting and worlds away from my childhood days when our stories were muzzled and trampled and buried in mass graves. Everything goes well until the final reception before the banquet. But this is not a victim narrative. I claim full responsibility for the mess to follow, admit it's my own fault. You see, I read too many books on how to keep a relationship fresh. Maybe it's because I'm the older lady and I want to keep up with my Ute? Not that he ever complains. I've rebelled completely against my proper Dakota upbringing, ignored my mother's stories of our virgin societies and chastity oaths. I admit I'm saucy and like to play. I've behaved myself for three days of conferencing which is apparently my limit, so I'm ready for a little action.

I dress for the banquet in a fairly conservative purple spandex suit, but the flash of danger is the butterfly underneath, in my silk underwear

— a sex toy, one of those tiny vibrating contraptions you can trigger with a remote from sixty feet away. I press the small black box into Quanah's hand as we make our entrance into the reception. At first he stares at the item in confusion, are we going to set off a bomb? So I whisper an explanation in his ear and wait for him to grin. He does. Gives a test hit of the switch. Warmth. Pleasure. I feel kissed by humming bees.

"Are you ready?" I ask him. He nods and we enter the social fray.

We mingle separately for a while, Quanah gravitating toward a knot of fellow graduate students while I rub shoulders with their professors. I am captured several times by fans, which is always nice, but then by a couple of men who are not my favorite people. First is Tom Ragsdale, a theologist turned Native Literature enthusiast who corners me the moment I'm alone.

"Diva! I have a question for you," he announces. I sigh inwardly but wait for him to continue. "After reading your book I'm very confused. You have characters practicing their Native religions, and some of them Christian ways, and still others are a combination of the two. So, tell me. What is the religion of most Indian people today?"

I stare at him with sizzling hostility, but he doesn't seem to notice. I'm usually more tactful, at least in professional settings, but I'm currently sipping a tall glass of a spectacularly smooth and dry Sauvignon Blanc. On an empty stomach. Tact has left the building.

"Please tell me you don't believe we're a monolithic people."

"What?" He's shredding the edges of a napkin that holds a slice of cheese. I watch, fascinated, waiting for the cheese to fall.

"Native Americans are an incredibly diverse group of people. In my family alone we practice several different spiritual traditions. I can't begin to answer your question. Imagine asking what the religion is of all Americans today. Some are Catholic, some are Jewish, some are Lutheran, some are Atheists, some are Buddhist, some are Dakota, and on and on. We're like that."

Tom squints at me in a cross way, as if I'm being argumentative for the sheer cussed fun of it.

"I get that, of course," he insists. "But generally-speaking. What religion are Indians?"

Quanah chooses this moment to trigger my little pleasure device so, annoyed as I am, it's all I can do not to moan in the man's face. I chew the inside of my mouth instead. I notice Quanah lifting his iPhone to take a photograph of me in my helpless state, and my breath hitches. *Oh no you don't*, I'm thinking, *Tom momentarily forgotten. Baby or not, you share that thing on*

Facebook and I'll block your ass, is what I'll tell him as soon as I can shake off this misguided soul.

I summon what discipline I can from the depths of my being, and, using my wine glass for emphasis, tell him for a final time: "I cannot answer your question. Each family and band and tribe is very diverse. We represent a myriad of beliefs."

I can't believe it. Tom persists. He speaks slowly now as if our problem has to do with language skills. "I know that. But surely you can generalize. As a group, what is your religion?"

I take a sip of wine to calm myself. It doesn't work. Perhaps the hidden butterfly I'm wearing has loosed more than my desire. I'm a channel of impatient noisy feelings, no safe middle-ground to be had in this passionate structure known as Diva. So I lean in to my antagonist's broad face, so close his nervous hand and the napkin of cheese brush against my breast. I lower my voice to make private the threat I have never openly said to anyone before, merely thought: "Stop, or I will hurt you."

Tom Ragsdale gasps and steps back, finally dropping the wedge of cheese. He can't seem to find a single word to express his reaction. I think he finally heard me.

I stalk off to punctuate my point and make a dramatic exit but Quanah hits the button again and zaps me, so I falter and have to lean against a wall. That's where Rick Marshall finds me. He's a non-Indian expert on the symbology of the Trickster Figure in Native texts who never met an Indian woman he didn't like.

"Diva," he coos, "you're looking well. You are going to get me an advance copy of your new novel? Tell me you are, don't play with my affections."

I duck my head in a half-nod, Quanah is really laying on the buzzer. I melt against the wall, vulnerable, wine carrying the warmth of my desire to my toes and my fingertips, even the smooth edge of my long hair gushing down my back. I bite the rim of my wine glass, the click of my teeth noisy, so noisy in the void between exchanges with Rick. He senses my arousal and moves in for the kill.

His lips brush my ear as he whispers in a throaty voice: "Have you read my last paper? Sherman Alexie, the New Contrary – Trickster Figures in the Urban Milieu."

Quanah is merciless, why did I give him that thing? I'm kissed now by a swarm of bees; they quiver and hum, they taste my pollen, make slick honey of my soul. I shudder.

"Yes," Rick continues, his breath spilling into my ear. "Send me your latest work and I'll deconstruct you chapter by chapter, paragraph by paragraph. I'll write in your margins, I'll highlight your images, I'll research your references, I'll swallow your poetry!"

In a sudden spasm of wrenching pleasure I drop the wine glass to the floor where it shatters to dust. I turn my face to the wall and lean my forehead against its cool surface. The buzzing stops. My body is quiet. Has the entire room gone quiet as well? I'm afraid to turn around and look.

The last thing I hear before slumping to the ground in a dead faint is Quanah's voice, loud with irritation: *"Hey, you, get your hands off my Auntie!"*

*

I'm more famous now than I was before, at least in Native circles. I don't think anyone will forget that reception at the Mystic Lake Casino. I get more fan mail from Native men, and can track how our gossip trails spread my story from region to region by checking the postmarks on the envelopes that come to me from nearly every reservation, excepting Hopi territory. No one dares tell my mother of my little misadventure, so in her eyes my dignity shines forth in fine Dakota fashion. But I know better. It will be a thousand years before I live this one down. Indians, as my mother is so fond of saying, have memories like elephants. We. Never. Forget.

Odds are you in the future have heard a version of this tale, so I want to set the record straight. Was I a little bit foolish in pursuit of love? Maybe yes. Did I damage my relationship with the young Ute dancer? Not at all. Now he's famous, too. But as this is partly a history lesson, I need to be serious for a moment.

I am a Native woman who was told all my life what this meant. I'm the object of projections and delusions, fantasies and violence; dead, never alive, dreamed, never known. But these are my pages so I am wresting the rules from the powers that be and making them up as I go along.

I am my own story, my own dream. I am present tense, not past perfect. My culture isn't lost in a grave but bursting from the keys of this computer, though it might look different from the way it did when my grandmother was born. I am allowed change. Change is the cold river that shocks us all. Sometimes it drowns us, pulls us away from where we want to be. Sometimes its water is the snap we need to wake us up and move us in better directions. Experts will tell you who I was, when I lived, when I died, but don't you believe them. I am not gone until I say I am.
I am still here.

Mark Childress
Nixon In Jackson

The day was weatherless: a flat gray sky and no wind. A policeman directed us to the far side of the parking lot to join the other bands.

We buttoned our uniform jackets, snapped the chin straps on our bearskin hats. With those other bands in view, we knew Mr. Waxman would not want us coming off the bus in anything less than full parade dress. Columbus and Warren Central were two of the best bands in the state, but today, miraculously, we would all be one band, playing the same welcoming march for the President.

Before I got off the bus I saw Waxman had already found the other band directors and was rocking back on his heels, laughing at something one of them was saying. It must be a big deal for him to stand alongside those men from the A-Division schools.

The other bands milled about with their uniform jackets off, snapping pictures of each other in front of the Coliseum. Lionel Wooten took one look at those half-dressed slobs and whistled us into four precise ranks, perfectly silent, standing at crisp attention. We knew what Lionel was thinking: show these rubes with their overgrown twohundred-piece bands how a real band behaves in the big city.

Lionel flashed his glittery mace, bit off three chirps on his whistle, and marched us in parade cadence (drums clicking sticks on the rims) to an exact halt just behind the chatting band directors. They had no choice but to turn around and appreciate us.

A burst of whistle. "Band!" Lionel boomed. "Attennn-hut!"

Waxman was delighted by our display of spontaneous flash. You could see on his face how he loved us for doing it. The other band masters started yelling at their bands to get it together and follow the example of Minor High, who don't need anybody to tell them to form up for God's sake!

Cecilia Karn gave us an E to tune by. Before long we were lined up as one band. We ran through a parking-lot rehearsal of "Hail to the Chief" at the hands of the Warren Central band director, a grouchy old man with a gray beard. He thrashed through the tune in such a hurry we could barely keep up. Waxman and the Columbus director huddled, then came back and asked if we could try it once a little slower. Warren Central handed Waxman the baton, and there was our own Waxman at the podium, leading two of the three best bands in Mississippi (and us!) at an easier tempo. "Hail to the Chief" never sounded so good.

A wide door rolled open just for us. We marched from daylight into the vast gloom of the Coliseum. Lionel halted us inside while the Secret Service looked us over. Men with crewcuts whispered into walkie-talkies and waved us through. Someone opened a rope. We passed through a corridor of steel barricades across the arena floor.

The Coliseum seemed enormous, jammed with schoolchildren all the way to the top, sending a cloud of chatter rising to the pleated ceiling. The place was full to the nosebleed seats, beyond even where we had to sit for Sonny and Cher.

I bet they lured Nixon to Mississippi with a firm guarantee, one Coliseum full of wildly cheering citizens to take your mind off Watergate. Then when things got to looking sketchy for the turnout, the governor emptied the schools and bused in all the children of Jackson. I saw whole sections of kids six and seven years old who could no more name the President than they could do differential equations, but when the teachers told them to yell for the President, they yelled their little heads off. They sent a big noise up into that vast bright space.

On the main floor were thousands of normal Mississippians who had come to see the President, to cheer him through his tough times. We all knew the world Nixon was living in now – Haig, Mitchell, and Dean, Judge Sirica demanding the tapes, Senator Sam Ervin, Haldeman and Ehrlichmann, Archibald Cox, and the Washington Post. What's wrong with wanting to come down to Mississippi where the people will still cheer for you? The more Nixon pisses off the rest of the country, the more Mississippi loves him. We love anybody in trouble, especially trouble of their own making, because down here we've all gotten in trouble and wished for somebody to give us a break.

The huge stage of Sonny and Cher had been replaced with a simple platform, a blue fabric backdrop, a spotlighted Presidential Seal. Some old man was making a speech in an irritating drone rendered inaudible by the PA system. Everyone in the Coliseum was busy ignoring him. A Secret Service agent walked us right in front of the podium while the man was speaking. I thought he was going to leave us there, but instead he herded us to a roped-off portion of the grandstand, behind and to one side of the stage. We had a clear view of the podium and the back of the old man's bald head.

The crowd chatted and waited. When you're waiting for the President nothing else matters very much, certainly not the warm-up speaker filling the air with his blather. You're looking at the Secret Service agents, dozens of them in dark suits muttering into walkie-talkies and gazing suspiciously upon the crowd. They hardly glanced our way; I suppose our band uniforms made us a semi-official part of the background.

I thought how easy it was to kill John F. Kennedy, even easier to kill Martin Luther King, and Bobby the easiest of all. If I had a gun right now I could shoot Richard Nixon from here. If I knew how to shoot, I could guarantee to kill him. I wondered if everybody has these thoughts or just Oswald, James Earl Ray, Sirhan Sirhan, and me.

Who would weep for Nixon? Tricia and Julie. Maybe Pat. (Probably not.)

Waxman paced the empty bench in front of our bleachers, cracking gum at the side of his mouth. I felt a hand on my shoulder. Brian Fairchild smiled in the vicinity of my ear. "Hey, Musgrove, I got what you ordered. Put your hand behind you."

I did as I was told. He slid a large sheet of cardboard between my fingers.

"Careful," he said. "Don't show it. Slide it down by your feet."

"What is it?"

"Guess," he said, moving off down the row for his next quiet conversation.

I managed to get the cardboard in front of me and tucked behind my knees without showing the world. I feigned dropping my glockenspiel mallet and while down there retrieving it I examined the posterboard, about two feet square, with a big black "Z" Magic-Markered on it.

Okay Brian. What are you up to? I leaned back to see him at the end of the row, whispering to Ted Herring, who was smiling and nodding. Two people down from me, Mindy Maples examined a cardboard square with a big black "O" on it.

"Mindy, what are we doing?"

She grinned. "You're so smart, Daniel. It's the greatest idea!"

Just then the lights failed, all at once – the children screamed, really screamed like in a funhouse and that brought a wave of laughter from the rest of the audience.

A spotlight played on one of the passageways to the right of the stage. In front of us in the dark, all three band directors gesticulated wildly, trying to get their bands' attention. Someone found a flashlight, switched it on, held its beam on Waxman as he counted us off.

First the trumpets' ruffles and flourishes, then Hail to the Chief:
BUM bum ba-BUM bum ba-BUM ba BUM ba da da
It was not as good as outside, but good enough. Here came a

tiny waving man in a dark blue suit, and yes that was him by the roar that went up. The spotlights found him and fixed him in their brilliant shafts of light. It says a lot for the power of spotlights that Nixon's entrance was one of the most dramatic things I'd ever seen. There he was, leader of the Free World, the biggest crook ever to occupy the White House. Here I was straining to hit the right notes on my glockenspiel while some hidden citizen within me felt a strong urge to leap up and cheer the President. There was something so exciting about seeing the most famous and powerful man in the world.

But that little waving man wasn't just the President, he was Richard Nixon. As far from Bobby Kennedy as you could get, and still be a person. I felt disgusted with myself. I stuck my mallet in my pocket. I withdrew the tinkling chime of one glockenspiel from the celebration of Nixon.

He held his hand up in that familiar hunchbacked wave of thanks, like a million times on the news. The awkward angle of his arm made his jacket ride up over his face while he ambled along waving, thanking the crowd. He took his time, drinking in the admiring roar and the firing of hundreds of Instamatic flashbulbs in the darkness. Any one of them could be a rifle shot, I thought. Any one of them could put an end to this show.

Nixon got this big dumb grin on his face when he passed in front of the band section – maybe the sight of our uniforms took him back to his college days, who knows? His face lit up with this sad, affectionate look, and he waved himself crazy waving at us.

He stepped up on the stage. Everyone got to their feet applauding. Nixon looked slightly younger and more agile than on TV. His face was not just a mask – he changed when he saw us! He became a human being, just for a moment, until the crowd called him on.

That surprised me. I didn't expect it.

He stood at the podium nodding and making half-hearted attempts to dampen the celebration. When the crowd began to cheer itself out, he said, "Governor Waller, all the distinguished guests on the platform, all of the distinguished guests in this audience. In answer to that very generous introduction by the Governor, I can only say that I am proud to be the first President in history to address the Mississippi Economic Council, and after this kind of a reception, I am sure I won't be the last one to do it."

The crowd laughed generously. He was speaking on the same PA as the mumblemouthed Governor, but the cadence of Nixon's voice was so smooth and familiar that even those of us sitting behind him could make out every syllable. Each applause line came back from the faraway ceiling with its own nicely enhancing echo. This was a man who knows how to speak to big crowds.

I felt a hand tugging my shirtsleeve – Mindy whispered, "Get ready."

"For what?"

"Your sign! Keep your eye on Brian."

"As a matter of fact," Nixon said, "as I looked at this huge auditorium, I thought I had never spoken in a place where I had so many people behind me."

The spotlights swiveled toward us. Brian Fairchild called "Now!" and stood up with a cardboard square in his hands. Mindy Maples jumped up with hers. So did Shanice James, and Jackie Williams, and David Watson, Melanie Singleton, Cecilia Karn, Terry Banks, Woody Foster, Larry Smith.

NIXO GO HOME

is what we spelled out until Mindy said "Daniel, hold it up!" and I held up my posterboard square so that we spelled

NIXOZ GO HOME

until I realized what an idiot I am, and turned the letter to make it say

NIXON GO HOME.

Flashbulbs flashed. Nixon turned to wave at us. He was wearing his President mask again, none of this human stuff now. He waved and turned back to his microphone. I don't think he even registered our sign.

But the other band directors did, and then Waxman, oh the horror that swept him. For an instant he was staring right at me with the N in my hands. He came scrambling toward us, hands windmilling in air, snatching my N and the O from Mindy Maples and H from Woody Foster and G from Terry Banks, frantically whispering "Give them here – give them to me!" His panic was real.

Sheepishly everyone handed over the signs. Mindy tried "sorry, Mr. Waxman," but he cut her off with two curt words.

Nixon plowed on with this speech: "And I want to pay tribute, incidentally, to your many guests, I understand, from the schools, the colleges, the other fine institutions. Particularly, I thank the Columbus, Warren, and Moran High School bands for playing 'Hail to the Chief'." Again a friendly wave in our direction.

Moran?

How can you look at a piece of paper that says MINOR and come up with Moran? It was one step short of Moron. Nixon kept going, no worse for wear.

The fuming Mr. Waxman placed our posterboard squares on his

folding chair and conspicuously sat on them.

We giggled and winked and high-fived behind the others' backs. I felt a flash of doubt before we did it, but Brian Fairchild impressed me with the smooth way he pulled it off. He moved too quickly to give us time for second thoughts, and he chose the exact moment Nixon when turned to face us. We did it, people saw us, it was over, no harm done. Waxman was pissed but he would get over it. And we had bragging rights for life! We told the President to get lost!

The speech turned dull and went on forever. Nixon talked about Senators Stennis and Eastland, America's will and determination and sense of destiny carrying us forward into great advances unforeseen at the present time, the end of World War II, his memories of Korea, social unrest, law and order, the great compromise of 1856, the meetings he'd just had with the Prime Minister of Great Britain, the President and Prime Minister of Italy, the Chancellor of Germany, and the President of France. He took a long detour through the economy, talking about the dip and the curve and the prognosis and all the new housing starts. For a while he talked about China. I lost the thread because I was focused on Mr. Waxman who was still enraged at the ten of us – at the whole band by association. Turning every so often to shoot a furious look of wait-till-I get-you-home over his shoulder.

Some Secret Service men came over and asked a few questions of the band director from Warren Central, who pointed to Waxman, and they talked to him, and one of them was looking directly at those of us who held up the letters in NIXON.

I wanted to tell Waxman that yes, it was my original idea but I didn't mean it literally, I didn't know Brian would actually go make the signs. When he handed me one I didn't know what it was. . .oh who am I kidding? He'll never believe me. I barely believe myself.

Nixon talked about turning the pages of history, the Forum at Rome, the march of civilization, and what it all means. He assured us that whatever the handwringers and the doomcryers say, the spirit of America is strong here in Mississippi. He talked about Gulfport after Camille, how he met a little girl with her two front teeth out who showed him what that American spirit truly meant.

"We often think that we live in the worst of times," Nixon said.

"And we do, thanks to you," I said under my breath. Mary Maher laughed.

"We often think, wouldn't it be better if we lived someplace else or were born at a different time?"

"Any other time would be nice," I said.

Mary said, "Shhh."

"Let me say to this younger generation, don't ever buy that, not about America, not about yourself, and not about the time in which you live, because you have a great future."

Yeah right. Thanks to you nobody will ever trust a President again. Nixon, go home . Go home and take your Presidential Seal with you.

The speech wound up with a bunch of patriotic blither about the critical leadership of this generation, twenty-five years from now it will be the year 2000 and the "four billion people of the Earth will look at America, will look at what we have done, and joining with us, they will say, 'God Bless America'."

With a wave he stepped back from the podium. He inhaled the answering roar of the crowd, mixed with a note of relief that he was done.

He turned to shake hands with the old goats lined up behind him on the stage. His speech had sent them into fits of joy, or so it seemed from the vigorous, almost spastic way they pumped his hand and grinned at him. It was fascinating to see the power invested in this normal-looking man who had that particular bulldog set to the jaw and the Fred Flintstone permanent five o'clock shadow. Nixon was a man like any other, and yet he held the great power of the world in his hands. One of those black suits carried a briefcase that could blow us all to heaven if necessary.

Another sign of his great power was how quickly he vanished – poof! Gone. Whisked out of there so fast he might have never been there at all.

The lights came on – everyone started and blinked. The schoolkids, freed from their hour-long prison of silence, sent up an ear-shattering cloud of noise.

Waxman stood with his head down. He was currently receiving a lecture from the Warren Central band director, the old man who had rehearsed us too fast. I wandered up to hear the man say, "If you have no more control over your students than that, you ought to get out of the business."

"Well sir, actually I'm proud of the job I do," Waxman said. "Don't you think the same thing could have happened to you?"

"Not in a million years. My students know what I would do to anyone who pulled a stunt like that."

"What's would you do?" Waxman said.

"Expel them. Not suspension. Expulsion. For Christ's sake, Bernie, it was the President of the United States!"

"He didn't actually see it, I don't think," Waxman said reasonably. "Do you?"

A cold finger ran a line down my neck. I did not like the sound of Expelled.

Because after all it was my idea. I could try my best to explain how Brian Fairchild had taken a passing remark and blah blah who would ever believe me? I was doomed.

I thought about making a run for it but how could I get away from here, who could I call? It wouldn't be too hard to track me down in my band uniform.

"Doesn't matter whether he saw it," Warren Central was saying. "The photographers saw it. The TV cameras saw it. I bet you make the national news with this one."

"Don't say that!"

"Sorry, Bernie, but you've embarrassed the hell out of all of us today! I just hope our program doesn't get tarred by what your idiot children did."

"Wait, Fred – "

The old man sloughed him off and stalked away. Waxman stood watching him go.

I did not want to be the one standing there when he turned around. I pulled my bearskin low over my eyes and tried to work myself back into the general muddle of the band.

"Musgrove." He was right behind me.

I turned. He held the stack of posterboard cards in his hands. "I believe you were holding one of these?"

"Yes sir," I said. Busted. No way out. God help me.

"Who else?"

Oh God. Oh no. He wants me to name names? Okay. Well. I have no choice. Only one thing to do.

"Mr. Waxman," I said. "It was all my idea."

"Aw now, wait a minute, don't go hogging the credit." Brian Fairchild stepped out of the crowd. "It was me, Waxman. Musgrove had nothing to do with it. I made those signs and passed 'em out and told 'em when to hold 'em up."

"Thank you, Brian," said Waxman. "Who else?"

One by one the conspirators edged forward. Only half of us were white. It occurred to me that Waxman should be glad to see the two sides of the band working together. We had achieved real integration, two sides coming together to deliver one message without even thinking about what color we were.

Waxman paced in front of us. "Musgrove, Karn, Foster, Banks – my seniors. God, am I disappointed. My seniors. You're supposed to set the example for the young ones. Instead you're thinking up a way to publicly insult the President. Did you think that was a good idea?"

Once again I appointed myself spokesman. "I did."

He whirled on me. "You did."

"I'm sorry, Mr. Waxman. But he only came down here because there's nowhere else he can go where they don't hate him. I don't care if he is the President, he's a crook. He's lying to the whole country. You know it. You probably hate him too, you just can't say it 'cause you're a teacher."

"Don't lecture me, Musgrove," he snapped. "When the hell did you. . .idiot children decide that the band is the place for your political statements and racial demonstrations and non-violent whatever the hell it is! This is my band and you're not going to use it that way!"

"It's a free country, Mr. Waxman." I climbed all the way up on my high horse. "Or least it's supposed to be."

Brian Fairchild said, "Come on, Mr. Waxman, it was a joke. It's over. It's not such a big deal, I bet Nixon is used to people holding up signs."

"You didn't have the Secret Service come asking you questions," Waxman sputtered. "They wanted all of your names. I should have turned you in. Fred Oakley says you should all be expelled. I guess we'll leave that up to Mr. Hamm."

"Mr. Waxman – "

"This is my reward? This is what I get for treating you like people, like friends? I give you free rein, I let you do what you want, I teach you how to get the best out of yourselves – and this is how you repay me?"

In my mind I saw a photograph on the front page of the Jackson *Clarion-Ledger*. When it came the next morning it was just as I had imagined it, splashed across the front page, beside the headline "President Speaks To Forum." The caption said, "Some Minor High School students welcomed President Nixon to the Mississippi Coliseum Tuesday with a gesture of defiance."

The familiar Nixon profile in focus. Our faces were fuzzy little dots. You would never be able to tell who was who. But our message came through loud and clear.

NIXOZ GO HOME

Jodi Angel

To The Gills

for James Thunder

The hooker had been living with us for three days before my father pulled me aside for the talk.

"I gotta talk to you for a minute, Benny."

I was standing in the kitchen, pouring cereal into a plastic container that had once held deli potato salad, and we were out of milk and there was nothing worse than spooning up bites of dry Captain Crunch, and I knew the roof of my mouth was going to take a beating.

My father pulled a soft pack of Pall Malls from the front pocket of the work shirt he still wore despite the fact that he was cashing his unemployment checks down at the EZ Mart, and he used to smoke Camels, but those were two bucks more a pack and we were Old Mother Hubbarding it in the long stretches between. He cleared his throat and ran his thumb across the wheel of a plastic lighter that refused to give up a flame and I listened to the hollow clicks.

"Misty would feel more comfortable if you started calling her mom," he said. My father was not a tall man, but he was solid and had once punched his fist through a bedroom door, and as he stood there in front of me, I could see that some slack had settled in.

I dug a wooden spoon into the cereal and tried to chew a big bite, but my spit was sucked up so fast that I was left with nothing but a mouth full of sharp dry grit. Misty came into the kitchen then, as if she had been waiting in the wings, and I noticed that she was also wearing one of my father's old work shirts over a pair of cutoffs that were so short that the pockets were rabbit eared out the bottom, and there was a smell to her, eucalyptus and sharp, something like a wrestling match or a warm locker room, and I realized what it was, Icy Hot, and the smell of muscle strain.

She opened the refrigerator, checked inside, hung on the door and looked over the edge at my father. "We need liquor, Martin," she said. "And I like fresh vegetables. And steaks. Those thick ones—what do you call them?" She closed her eyes and thought for a second, snapped her fingers as though the friction might kick her memory loose. "Rib eyes. That's it. I need protein, Martin." She smiled at my father, and swung on the refrigerator door, and I could feel the cold air rolling out, and as my grandmother used to say, "somewhere a penguin was dying," and I thought about saying that to Misty, but I knew it wouldn't matter much to her.

My father finally got the lighter to do something more than dry fire, and he sucked the Pall Mall to life, exhaled, walked over to Misty and kissed her loudly on the cheek. "Write it down, baby," he said. "Make me a list. I'll get you whatever you want."

"We need milk," I said.

Misty looked at me and shut the refrigerator door. "It's my list," she said. "Mom makes the list."

On the fourth day that the hooker had been living with us, me and my buddy Norman were up in my room, stretched out on my worn carpet, smoking my father's Pall Malls and debating over who had the better album cover—Pink Floyd's Wish You Were Here or Led Zeppelin I, and we were getting pretty heated because there was a lot to like about people on fire or shit blowing up.

"I bet Misty's a cokehead," I said.

"Snowblind," Norman said. "Hittin' the gutter glitter. Chalked up." He took a long drag on the cigarette and then exhaled quickly. "She rides the lightning. Double bubbles. She's probably snortin' the yayo." We both watched the smoke catch the light. "Cum catchers are always strung out," he said.

"Yayo? What the fuck is that?"

"C'mon. Antonio Montana? Scarface? You know your dad has already introduced Misty to his little friend."

Me and Norman had been buddies since the third grade, and he had been doing my Algebra homework since October, and he had a great head for plans when there was nothing much to do. I knew there was a strong chance that he would get a car before I ever did, and he liked what I liked, so all in all he was a good friend to me.

There was a soft knock on my door and I turned the volume down on my stereo, just as Getty Lee was gonna tell us why they called him a workin' man, and I said "yeah," and my father pushed the door open and came in.

"Misty wants you to read these," he said.

He handed me a stack of brochures. On the cover of the top one was a picture of a bunch of guys in camouflage, holding machine guns and cutting across white caps in a black rubber boat and below that it said: There are jobs. And then there's the Marine Corps.

"She wants you to plan for your future," my father said. "She said you don't even have to finish high school. You can start making good money right now."

I looked down at the glossy pictures. The paper felt sticky.

"Maybe I want to go to college," I said.

"Misty says there's no good jobs out there. Look at me. I lost my good job." He pointed down at the brochure. "This is a career. This is security," he said. "Misty says the future is now."

"You delivered furniture," I said. "I'm sure the field is wide open."

Norman looked up at my father. "It smells good downstairs," he said. "What is that? Steak?"

"Misty's making some kind of thing," my father said. "She likes to cook. She just doesn't like to eat much."

I could hear Norman's stomach growling from where I sat. "How long before dinner?" I asked.

"Nah, this ain't for you. Twenty-seven-dollars worth of steaks? I ain't wasting them."

Norman crushed his Pall Mall out into an empty cereal bowl by my bed. "Are those my cigarettes?" my father asked.

Norman waved his hand around to clear out the smoke. "I don't think so, sir."

"Misty says you're bleeding me dry around here, Benny. I gotta tell you that. I'm startin' to feel the pinch." He left the room and shut the door behind him.

On the fifth day that the hooker had been living with us, I was standing in the kitchen, staring out the sliding glass door at the piss yellow lawn, watching a squirrel trying to dig something out of the dirt, and I was tapping the last of the crumbs out of a Pringles can when she came up behind me, slid up like a shadow, and I didn't even know she was there until I felt her breath on the back of my neck.

"You ever have your dick sucked, Benny?" she asked.

I lowered the can from my mouth and licked the salt off of my lips. "Yeah," I said.

"Liar." The smell of Icy Hot stung my eyes and there was something underneath, something like gasoline or exhaust fumes, and she was still in my father's work shirt, the one that said "Martin" in a patch over the pocket, and "F&S Furniture" on the back, and I wanted to step past her but she was too close and the sliding door was shut behind me, and I pressed myself against the glass.

"You never had your pole smoked? Your knob jobbed? Chrome polished? Piston played? Dome blown? Sword swallowed? Sausage gargled? Had someone play the skin flute? Honk bobo's nose? You've never been brained? Had lipstick on your dipstick?" She took a step backward and looked me up and down. "You've never served up some throat yogurt?"

I just stared at her.

"Fifty dollars," she said.

On the sixth day that the hooker had been living with us, my father's drinking buddy, Paulie K., stopped by. I was standing over the sink, eating cold Chunky soup from the can, and they were sitting at the table, blowing through some Pabst, and both of them were watching Misty through the open slider as she bent over so that the ragged bottoms of her cutoffs slid back over the white skin crescent of her bare ass while she planted pink flowers in a narrow stretch between the cement patio and the lawn.

"I like to do things with my hands," she said. My father had bought her new shoes, leopard print with high heavy soles and she was out in the yard in them now, gardening.

"She's a fucking catch, Martin," Paulie K. said. He took a long swallow without moving his eyes from Misty.

My father leaned back in his metal chair and raised the front two legs from the floor so that the chair groaned under his weight. "She's a god-damn prize, is what she is," my father said. He drained his beer and fished another one from the busted open case they had on the floor between them.

Outside, the sun came out from behind a cloud and lit up the back-yard in watery April light and Misty looked over her shoulder toward the house, legs straight and calf muscles bunched tight as fists as she bent over the half dozen flowers in the dark and torn up patch of dirt.

"You better put on a ring it," Paulie K. said. "Possession is nine-tenths of the law."

On the seventh day that the hooker had been living with us, my father went out to run errands for Misty, and I got her to wait for me upstairs in my room, blindfolded.

"Kinky costs more," she said. "Seventy-five."

"Fine," I said.

When she was on her knees, I dropped the blinds and turned out the lights, and Norman slid into the room as I went out, and I shut the door behind me. I pressed my ear so tight against the wood that I forced a splinter into my cheek, and even though I couldn't hear much, I could hear enough, and I couldn't help but get hard and wish I'd just said fuck it and let it be me, and when it was over, Norman came out, red-faced and smiling, pulling up his zipper, and looking ten pounds lighter and four years older than he did before he went in.

"How was it?" I asked.

"Seriously?" he said, and even his voice sounded deeper.

On the eighth day that the hooker had been living with us, she confronted my father in the living room.

"Benny owes me seventy-five dollars," she said.

My father hit the mute button on the TV and dropped the smoldering end of a Camel into one of the empty Heineken bottles lined up on the table beside him.

"What?" he said.

"Benny owes me seventy-five bucks. He won't pay up."

"Pay up for what?"

"I *serviced* him, Martin, Jesus, and he won't pay me what he owes."

My father looked at me. I shrugged my shoulders. "I don't know what she's talking about."

"Is this fucking true?" he said.

I was kicking Norman's ass at chess, and he looked up. His face was as empty as his side of the board, but inside I knew that he was probably thinking about the warmth of her mouth and the fact that he had gotten his dick sucked by a hooker for free.

"She's probably coked out of her mind," I said. "She doesn't know what she's talking about."

"Strawberry girl," Norman said.

"He's full of shit, Martin," Misty said. "I don't do drugs." She rubbed the back of her hand under her nose and sniffed loudly, twice, left nostril, then right. "He asked me for it, Martin. It was just a job."

My father looked around the room. It was hot and there were too many smells—muscle rub, garlic, old steak, stale beer, sweat, and musk, all hanging in the air like dirty sheets.

"Prove it," I said.

Misty looked at me. "You little fucker."

"C'mon, dad," I said. "She has to be thinking about somebody else," I shook my head. "It wasn't me." I hadn't called my father "dad" in about three years and the word had a tangy taste to it. It rolled off my tongue like a thick wad of phlegm.

Norman was still bent over the chess board, trying a half-hearted attempt at the Boden's Mate that he could never pull off, and I watched him struggle to line up the bishops again.

"He ain't cut, Martin," Misty said. "He had me blindfolded, but there's no mistaking that feeling in my mouth. He's got an anteater. A banana skin." She pointed at me. "A blind fuckin' chicken neck."

My father stood up and I could see sweat standing out on his forehead. "Blindfolded?" He rubbed at his temples and he left two hard red spots high up on his cheeks. "Wait a minute. Benny ain't uncircumsized."

I cleared my throat. "What about Paulie K.?" I asked.

My father paused in mid-drink and what was left in his Heineken spilled over the lip and onto the carpet and splashed back against the cuffs of his Chinos. "Son of a bitch," he said.

Things happened all at once, and there was some crying, and somebody knocked into the chess board and Norman's big move was lost in the shuffle, and when Misty came back down stairs, she had a little make up case with her and a pair of broken sandals hanging from her hand.

"You came with nothing and you'll leave with nothing," my father said.

"Can you at least get me a bus ticket?"

I had expected more crying and carrying on, and maybe some begging with Misty back in her favorite position, and working some carpet dirt into the creases of her knees, but in the end she didn't seem too broken up about being told to pack it up and go. She was used to shelf life, expiration dates, and boredom had a flavor that probably tasted a lot like Pabst.

"At least give me a ride to the bus station, Martin," she said again, and my father snapped another beer open, set it back on the table, thought better of it, and then emptied it in three quick swallows.

"Sure, okay," he said. "I guess."

After they left, Norman and I finished off my father's beers and even though we didn't talk about it, I knew that Norman knew that things between us wouldn't be quite right until I got what he had already had, and considering that sophomore year had turned out to be one long empty stretch of tease, it might be junior year before the playing field got evened again.

Outside it was dark and the air was thinner without the benefit of sun, and I opened the back sliding door to empty the house of the smells, and I knew that Misty had the whole city in front of her now, belly-up and spread open under the stars, and my father was taking her across it, guiding his beat up Pontiac through the bright and shiny center where even the street corners were full of possibility, and for a little while my father had had a dream again that in reality had about as much substance as smoke, and Norman had crossed a line that nobody else could see, and I poured Captain Crunch into a coffee cup and chewed without thinking, and didn't feel anything at all because I wasn't sure about what exactly had been left for me.

Casey Haynes

Honest Work

The monks on stage, standing stiff and upright and even-spaced as new fence posts, raised their voices and filled the place with a deep gut rumble. A higher pitch wove through the tumbling throat singing, and the sounds together gave Mark a weird tingle in his shoulders. He didn't usually question art, but he might not have distinguished the noise from a bunch of leaf blowers if he wasn't sitting all slicked up in a dark theater.

He considered leaning over to Melanie and saying as much but thought better of it. Mark figured his imitation of a leaf blower would be pretty sorry, and she seemed caught up in the performance. This was the third she'd taken him to, and she was pretty insistent about calling them performances, he noticed, never shows. Shows were what your little cousins put on at the First Baptist around Christmas time.

Mark thought it a little bit ridiculous that people made money telling stories or playing drums made from old appliances, but he shelled out to see them just the same. Melanie offered, even demanded, to pay for their tickets since she was dragging him along to them, but Mark was stubborn. He didn't make much money landscaping the campus, but that didn't matter. As a teenager Mark let his girlfriend pay for a date, and he'd had chivalry beaten into him when his father found out. His daddy wasn't cruel, but he did have a strong sense for what he called decorum. Now, Mark wouldn't date a girl if he couldn't cover her meal and movie ticket. In the end, he and Melanie often compromised, each paying for the other's dinner.

Mark felt Melanie's hand hovering over his and looked down from the men in the pastel robes. She often did this, not out of hesitation, but because she seemed to enjoy making him come to her. On a cool day in the early spring she had smiled at him as she walked past. He was planting a new row of dogwoods and nearly dropped one onto the guy digging the hole. He thought it was a fluke, but the pretty girl with the patched-up backpack kept passing and smiling as the months went by. Mark wasn't great with women, but neither was he hopeless; he could take a hint being served on a platter, and one day he set down his hedge clippers, laid his grimy gloves on top, and introduced himself.

Ever since, she'd met him halfway, though God knows why. He found out she wasn't some doe-eyed freshman with a hand-me-down backpack but a graduate student getting paid for bioinformatics research she did on the side. He understood the basic science she explained to him, and she barely spoke of her work beyond generalities, but things like this—performances—made him uncomfortable. Mark knew she could do better than a gardener from the mountains, and had before.

Mark took Melanie's hand as the last notes of the song seemed to settle over everything like a bed sheet, leaving an electrified silence in their wake. The half-dozen men bowed their heads and left the stage as if answering some call to action, and every person in the auditorium rose in applause.

"That was incredible," Melanie said as they stepped into the cool air of the October evening.

Mark buried his hands in the pockets of his denim jacket and watched bats fly drunk through clouds of moths and disappear into the darkness. They walked past the Belk tower, which was lit up from the base and looked to be brooding over most of the campus. Dew already settled on the grass he'd have to mow in the morning, and Mark tried to imagine the bats' inaudible, predatory chorus.

"I didn't know people could make noises like that," he said.

"You know," Melanie said, tracing the inside of Mark's bicep, "you'd be surprised at what the body can do."

Mark didn't know what to say. She'd do this too—say something that meant something else, but he was never sharp enough to come back with anything. Mark sat third wheel once to a conversation between Melanie and a professor at lunch, and it felt like he was watching a movie. The two went back and forth like they had been waiting their whole lives to say each line.

Normally, he'd just squeeze her hand or kiss her cheek in response, but this time he jangled his car keys and asked if she was ready to see her dad.

"Yeah, he's been clamoring to meet you for a while."

He figured her father probably knew little more than that his daughter was dating a guy from Facilities Management. And what else was there to know? Mark taught himself to throw playing cards and could bury one into an apple from ten feet back, but he didn't have much else he could put on a résumé. Granted, he didn't know much about the old man either except that his wife left him. She took off right before Melanie came to college, ran away with some lawyer from Raleigh. She wrote back only once, a letter with no return address which Melanie still kept. She had let Mark read it, but all he got out of it was that the lawyer had something special about him that Melanie's mother never knew she wanted until she found it.

Sounded like a bunch of crap to Mark, but he held Melanie tight to him afterwards.

Mark felt the cold ridges of his key as they approached his truck. The vehicle was old and needed work, but it still looked pretty. He'd washed and cleaned it out the day before, his tools in the bed and an air freshener in the cab. Mark went to the passenger side and opened the door, but Melanie kissed him and took the keys from his hand.

"Get in," she said. "It'll be easier if I drive us there."

"You sure?"

"Yup. It's not really close, and you'll miss it if you blink."

Melanie closed his door and seemed to skip around the truck to the driver's side.

"Plus," she said as she rocked the seat closer to the steering wheel, "I've never driven a truck before." She put the key in the ignition, shot him a wide, crazyeyed grin and revved the engine.

They drove slowly leaving the campus, and Mark admired the way the moonlight settled on the treetops like wax. The truck took a right on Harrison and sped through Charlotte. Mark believed the nicest part of the city was where you could forget it was a city. They often walked the paths that cut through the woods, and back in the summer they shared a first kiss in the Harwood Garden surrounded by azaleas the color of lipstick. As the headlights and streetlights flew by, Mark felt like the truck was hurtling along impossibly fast.

At a Shell station Mark got out and walked toward the store.

"Where are you going?" Melanie called from the window.

"I'm gonna get something to eat and take a leak," he replied, walking backwards as he spoke.

"Not in that order?"

"Not in that order," he said, smiling back to her.

Mark washed his hands and walked past rows of junk food. He pulled out his wallet and counted the bills—not enough to fill the tank but enough to get them there and buy a bag of chips for the road. He turned sideways past a homeless man in a scarf eyeing a candy bar and went to the register. He paid for the bag and then asked the lady if she could put the rest on pump six outside.

"The white Ford?"

"Yes ma'am."

She handed the money back to Mark. "It's already pumping sir, paid by card."

"What?"

But he didn't wait for her to answer. Mark barely registered the tinkle of the bell as he pushed the door open. Melanie was already returning the pump to its cradle.

"What're you doing?"

"I just thought I'd fill up since it's kind of a long drive out."

"You shouldn't have."

"It's no trouble, really."

"No. You should not have. It's my truck, dammit. I can buy my own gas."

Melanie's eyes held something like fire for a moment, then fell. "I'm sorry," she said. "I wouldn't have done it if I'd known."

She returned her gaze to his, steady as rope pulled taut, and waited. She was tougher than any girl he'd met, more than many of the men, too. Mark didn't make a habit of yelling at women, but on the occasions he felt he needed to, every one had broken down and he'd end up apologizing. Sometimes he forgot that he'd inherited his father's way of scolding, rare and matter-of-fact enough to make you feel you deserved what you got.

"You ready to head on out?" he asked finally.

"Yeah," she said. They got in the truck, and Melanie, hands on the steering wheel, looked at Mark. "So, what did you get from the store?"

He held his hands up as if expecting to find the chips there and then looked back through the barred window of the convenience store and saw the woman holding the bag he'd left on the counter. She handed it to the homeless man. Mark closed his eyes and breathed in the scent of pine needles and the sweetness of Melanie's perfume.

"I guess I forgot. Forgive me?"

"There'll be food at my dad's place," she said and winked. "You lucked out."

They drove, passing the suburbs, Mark noticed, and after that he had no idea where they were going. The digital clock on the dash was busted, so he couldn't tell how much time passed before they pulled into a wooded drive that became pitted gravel. They passed an old pickup sitting on cinder blocks, the grass around it having grown higher as if to shield it from view, and Mark thought about Melanie's mother. He wondered if she felt whisked away when she was with the smooth-talking lawyer. Mark could only imagine the sped-up city minutes sliding past those two like raindrops on a windshield.

Melanie pulled up to a singlewide nestled into one edge of a large clearing and parked. When the rattling of the engine died out, Mark heard dogs barking. He caught the keys as Melanie tossed them, and as soon as she cleared the door she loosed a whistle that echoed through the woods. Moments later two hounds burst from the darkness. They were light brown and lean-muscled and could have seemed threatening if they'd not immediately rolled to present their stomachs to Melanie.

"That you, Mel?"

The man stood in front of his open door, oblivious to the bugs flying into the trailer. Melanie's curled hair bounced as she rose from the dogs, who scrambled up after her.

"Yeah, Dad."

"Did you bring that boy of yours? Bring him on up."

Melanie smiled and reached for Mark's hand. They walked up the drive together, Melanie's father watching them the whole way from the edge of his porch. He was not a big man, but he looked tall in his work boots and the wife-beater he wore despite the cold.

"Floyd," he said, his hand straight out before Mark had gotten to the top of the steps. Floyd gripped firm and pulled as if Mark were in danger of falling into something only he recognized. "Damn good to meet you, son."

"Melanie told me all about you."

Floyd tilted his head. "She did, huh? Well that's nice." And then to Melanie, "It's good to see you too, hun. Come inside. I've got some beers."

"We can't drink, Dad. We've got to head back tonight."

"Then uh..." Floyd gestured with a Marlboro that appeared from nowhere.

"Mark," Mark said.

"That's right. Mark here will drink a few with me, and you can drive you both back," he said through the side of his mouth as he lit the cigarette. He turned to the porch light and blew smoke at a captured moth.

Mark looked at Melanie, but he couldn't read the stare she had fixed on her father.

"I appreciate it sir, but I can't have too many. I've got to be up early."

"I always thought a hangover once in a while'd teach you the value of doing work sober," Floyd said. "But fair enough, I suppose. Come on in."

The trailer was sparse, but still somehow seemed messy. Crumpled beer cans sat everywhere. The prominent piece of furniture was a patched-up sofa that still bled yellow foam. Only the big flat screen television seemed new, although a crooked set of bunny ears duct-taped to the top made it look even more out of place. Mark thought it felt like home. Floyd came from the kitchen with a metal fold-out chair, spun it around and sat down, motioning toward the sofa.

"So how'd you two meet?"

"Nothing too romantic," Melanie said, though she gave Mark's hand a squeeze. "I just saw Mark around campus a few times and he asked me out."

Floyd's eyes narrowed. "I thought Mel said you worked."

"I do, sir. On the campus trimming hedges and planting mostly. It's not real glorious stuff."

"It's honest work, son," Floyd said. "Nothing bad in honest work."

"Thank you," Mark said, "but it's nothing to what your daughter does. You told him about the grant, right, Melanie?"

"I heard about it," Floyd said and snuffed out his cigarette in a ceramic ashtray. "Some bigwig gave you fake money to throw around?"

"It was almost three hundred thousand dollars, Dad." Melanie said each number slowly as if to help him understand. "My team was awarded the money to expand on the results of the research we published a year ago."

"Yeah? And what was that exactly?"

"We rewrote algorithms for processing data," she began, her grip on Mark's hand tight. "We redefined the collation of bisulphite sequencing data; three papers on epigenetic DNA expression have already cited us."

At "DNA" Floyd leaned back, victory in his folded arms.

"So, little things," he said.

Melanie's lips tightened, but her grip went slack.

"That's all you ever done since your momma left," he continued. "You moved to that city and you can't think of nothing more sensible than pointing your face down a microscope all day."

"Floyd, I think we've gotta get going," Mark said, standing. "It's a hell of a drive home." Melanie didn't say anything, but neither did she resist when he tugged her up from the sofa.

Floyd glanced at Mark for a moment, then stood so quickly he knocked over his chair. "And you wonder why it is I don't seem proud of you."

Melanie took her coat from Mark and went straight for the door knocking Floyd and several of his empty beer cans out of the way. Mark began to follow when Floyd put a hand on his shoulder.

"I like you, boy, but you're making a mistake dating my daughter." He looked away then shook his head. "She don't know what she wants outta life. Why do you think she brought you here? Wasn't for chitchat and telling me about 'research money.'" Floyd let his hand drop from Mark's shoulder and stepped back. "Love her to death, but she knows I don't give a shit about that. Sad as it is to say, my guess is she figured I'd take a liking to you."

"Well," Mark said. He caught Floyd's stare and held it, "I hope you have." Mark offered his hand, but Floyd only looked at it.

"Heh, you're something else." Floyd turned away, adjusted the crooked antenna perched on his flat screen. "Some words of wisdom, free of charge? Anybody thinks they're better than you, tell 'em to fuck off—you don't need that."

Floyd reached for his beer but grabbed an empty can. "Well goddamn," he said as he tossed the can across the room. Mark closed the door behind himself while Melanie's father searched for a single, half-full Bud Light among the wreckage of his home.

Mark found Melanie propped against the truck. The dogs sat by her side, but she paid them no attention, so they bounded up to Mark. He patted them and stood in front of Melanie.

She didn't look at him for several seconds, just kept her gaze pointed toward the woods like something important lurked back there. Mark turned and leaned next to her.

"Sorry I dragged you all the way out here," she said. "You didn't need to hear that."

"It's fine," he said and opened the passenger door. "You show me to the highway, and I'll get us home."

They drove back in silence. Mark thought about biology; he didn't know much, but he knew about DNA, how things like eyes or ears passed down from parents to children. When Melanie, all stirred up one day, told him about epigenetics, she expected him to be surprised.

"It's not written on the nucleotide like some sort of stone tablet," she'd said. "We don't know much yet, but there's evidence methylation can carry behaviors from one generation to the next."

"Makes sense," Mark said. "My dad loves baseball, I do too."

"No, that's a part of nurture: your environment. Like I said, it's behaviors, states of mind, so many things the DNA can't account for, all of it being passed on somehow. Stressed out mice gave birth to stressed out mice, whether their parents were there or not."

"Maybe that's because you took their parents away," Mark said in a moment of thoughtlessness. She didn't talk to him about biology much after that. Mark thought of his own father. How much of Mark came from one lucky swimmer? What parts of him came from his father's hand?

Which ones came from the gnarled hands of a half dozen farmers before him? If what Melanie said was true, something else must weave through their lives like a second pitch whistling over a bass note. Mark watched the passing streetlights play warning flashes across Melanie's face. Somewhere in the distance a train bellowed into the night, and Mark tried to picture the bats careening silently overhead.

BOOK REVIEWS

DARK. SWEET. *New & Selected Poems* by Linda Hogan
Coffee House Press
Paperback, 419 pgs.
2014.
Reviewed by William Pitt Root

When Ezra Pound proclaimed poetry to be "news that stays news," he gave us a new standard as fresh now as the day it was declared. It struck a nerve of instant recognition in writers around the world and in many readers as well: it's impossible for what is new to stay new, and yet…. That paradox has long retained its place as a primary challenge, an impossible goal. Linda Hogan is among the very few poets I can think of who has so consistently, with so seemingly little strain, given us poem after poem, book after book, without a shred of rot for time to feast on nor any whiff of false sentiment to betray what is so clearly authentic in her works of prose or poetry.

DARK. SWEET. This is a title that both attracts and teases at first glance. Later, among the new poems, we will find the full title is "Dark. Sweet. The Full Eclipse" and then learn that in the complete darkness of that full eclipse the poet experiences a epiphany encoded in those two words. This New & Selected Poems generously collects her choice of works from her first collection, CALLING MYSELF HOME, and all the others from ECLIPSE, SEEING THROUGH THE SUN, SAVINGS, THE BOOK OF MEDICINES, ROUNDING THE HUMAN and a long work in the small, exquisite book called INDIOS. Her titles alone serve as signposts for her journey: returning to root sources, witnessing darkness, seeing through the very source of light, the collection of healing powers (often literal roots), and the task of rounding out the human in part by reacquainting what is human with what is other than human and celebrating both the differences and such crossovers as may bind us into the greater community of being, even without our being aware of such connection. Although thoroughly grounded she never shies away from the big questions.

THE WAY IN

Sometimes the way to milk and honey is through the body.
Sometimes the way in is a song.
But there are three ways in the world: dangerous, wounding, and beauty.

To enter stone, be water.
To rise through hard earth, be plant,
Desiring sunlight, believing in water.
To enter fire, be dry.
To enter life, be food.

The 400+ pages make this handsome book a hefty one as well, and yet the more one reads around among these poems the lighter the book feels in one's hands. The language in these poems is so shorn of what is dispensable (adjectives, adverbs, nearly very "this," "that," or "which," polysyllables of Roman origin, the fluff and kerfuffle of commerce, the pollutants of political distortion, dumb vulgarity) that it reminds me of the first time I saw hand-blown Murano glass figures on an island close to Venice. Figures of grace and transparency captured light that seemed immediately to intensify. But while her language is often elemental it is never elementary; she moves between the newest science and the oldest intuitions and wisdom tales at the same time as she moves easily from starkly direct speech to "tell it slant":

...and there is a feeling, too, of awe and respect,
and, yes, remorse
for our kind who have tried tor each heaven,
learn a universe
and found stars that swallow light,
that bounded darkness is a matter
between light and broken light,
and we don't even know
the animals that walk outside our sleep
yet we have raveled there so often
there are not so many of them now
where light falls across the hunting grounds
we call a world that's small
because we've matched it to ourselves
and with all the lies we tell ourselves
so we won't see the world collapse
but when it does
it is not from what is known
but from what is never seen.

[from "The Night Constant"]

Skimming the news over breakfast recently I learned it has just been discovered that a warp in space time has given one particular supernova a second, then a third chance to shine, using an entire galaxy as a gravitational lens. This validates what Einstein predicted almost a century ago. What has long been theory, referred to as the Einstein Cross, now is news because it has been elevated to fact. Because it has been confirmed by observation. We can see it. And this process has parallels to how poetry, I should say some poetry, such as the fragment above, moves from being words on a page to becoming stars that burn in the firmament of our spirits.

This poet, invitingly down to earth one moment, can also be dizzyingly unpredictable the next. Here are some opening lines of poems:

In the early morning
I forget I'm in this world.
    ["First Light"]

How is it decided
ho among us has hands,
gill slits...
    ["Dimensions"]

I like the smell of pine
In those rings
Of the axe
    ["Woman Chopping Wood"]

The men wore human skins
But removed them at night.
    ["Skin"]

Or this one, simple but evocative, which hardly could be more timely and yet is likely to remain "news" incident after incident for quite a while to come:

In this country,
The police shoot targets shaped like themselves.
Sometimes the targets shoot back.
    ["Neighbors"]

But for Linda Hogan criticisms are often building blocks of hope and that is the underlying theme of much of her work. Her book, introduced with a quote from Ron Hauschi that reads "To write poetry, I have to be in love with the world," is more generally dedicated "for the future of our world, for the indigenous people and all the others who care for our forests and the lands we want to keep whole." Hogan, who is of Chickasaw ancestery, also dedicates her work to the planet, "with its great waters, old-growth forests, and old-growth people, but also to our young," including her numerous grandchildren, various friends, and "for Jayla, great-grandchild who will inherit this future."

Linda Hogan is a powerhouse, a clear, fearless poet through and through—her birth name is in itself a poem, a vision and a promise. She is both the home of beauty and a beautiful home, refuge not only from ugly brutality but from vanity as well—free from society's false securities such as mere prettiness, which Rilke might well have said is the pettiness left over once the element of terror has been removed from beauty. She, like her work, is lean, beautiful, empowered, and hers is the unblinking eye of the artist aware. Aware not of this or of that but aware, as in being native to that state of being.

Here is the end of poem that closes this volume:

…unless we venture into the world
where we may find some cure for the present,
we will not know how far we have to go back
to speak once again with the animals,
to learn the song the first ones laid down
efore the holy me and history-lost women
were born to kindness among their own.
How far do we have to go, how far is it
to the holy springs, the first water,
the first bones of our creation,
to compassion for all in that beginning
human marrow?
       ["After Silence, Return"]

Habitation: Collected Poems by Sam Hamill
Lost Horse Press
624 pages $25 (paperback)
September 2014
Reviewed by Rebecca Seiferle

In "Lives of a Poet: A Letter to Gary Snyder," Sam Hamill writes, "a poet is one who recognizes sacramental relationships." In Habitation: Collected Poems sacramental relationships take many forms. These dialogical poems converse with and listen to the political world, to the beloved, to a much loved text that one is translating, to landscape, to the erotic body, to long held friendships, and to solitude and silence. Hamill's poems deepen "our engagement with all that is human." A richness of classical allusion situates each of Hamill's poems not only in its lyric moment but also in a historical and cultural context.

What is heard is most important here, the cadence of the voice finding its own language to express its habitation, on the earth, in the body. Hamill's voice, valuing the unadorned, is sometimes deceptively simple, but a closer listening reveals subtle and confident music. In "Lives of a Poet: A Letter to Gary Snyder," listen to how the sturdy "n's" and "r 's" of the first stanza are moved forward by the "s" of "passed since" and then carried forward in the "s" at the end of "mountains,'" "rivers," "poems." The line breaks, ending on the prepositions, "to," "of" further exert a syntactical pull onward.

Nearly forty years
have passed since Kenneth Rexroth
introduced me to
the mountains and rivers of
your poems, the campfire life

In the second stanza the poem flowers, into a kind of mysterious meadow, dark lit, alive with an inner gaze.

flickering softly
across a page of Milton
animal shadows
and wide, wise innocent eyes
observing from the darkness.

What creates that opening into the mystery is the poet's ear, attuned to the pitch of existence. the soft "o,'", the sound of the short "i" in "flickering" "animal" rising into the long "i" sound of "wide" "wise." The reader, too, has to stop and hear, in the Buddhist sense to *pay attention*. This kind of inner listening translated onto the page is undoubtedly informed by Hamill's many decades translating from Japanese and Chinese, tonal languages where a slight shift in pitch completely alters the meaning of a word.

Habitation spans decades of work, beginning with Hamill's earliest poems that evoke the Western landscape where he grew up. The language in these early poems is gritty, capturing perfectly the ruggedness of the environment where an "old black thunderhead/ lurcht down the western slope/ like a glacier/ with a continent in its teeth ("The Great Divide") or working farm life where "barns yawn immensely/cathedrals of the West, /temples of dung & animal sweat." Yet in evoking moments of sensory experience, Hamill's poems open into moments of inner seeing, as in "First Snow:"

What I have left undone
        I leave, undone,
a white silence
falling through the fields
where dark husks uselessly open.

Here, the "white silence" and "the dark husks uselessly open" have the gravity and stillness of being. I am reminded of how meditation as a practice is like Keats's negative capability accepting the binaries of existence without an irritable reaching after facts or meaning—a simple and difficult acceptance of what is. In this case we are the undone, the white silence, the falling, and the dark husks uselessly open.

It's difficult to do justice to the rich variety of the 604 poems in this monumental work. There are poems of sharp humor ("Testament of the Thief"), of bawdy homage, of "Sheepherder Coffee," of music and of cooking, and of deepening surprise. "Second Psalm" beginning with the question, first in Latin then in English, "How shall we sing the Lord's song in an alien land?" begins with a construction worker. We follow him through his daily routine, pulling on "the long woolen socks of his trade," and then hear the "bark of D8 Cat, diesel purr" which "buzzed inside his ears." This man who doesn't "remember the heron" or "the child laughing" finally hears, at the end of the poem, "faintly...the music of machine./ And all too soon he learns/ the terrible truths they sing." We hear them too, and are, unexpectedly, in the realm of the political and the historical.

One of the perpetual debates in American poetry concerns the politically, socially aware poem, and it's clear from Sam Hamill's work where he stands. I say American poetry because elsewhere in the world, writers and poets are considered to inevitably have a political and social role. For Hamill a political consciousness, a social conscience, is simply part of being a human being with all the experiences of living in the world. Many of Hamill's poems are addressed or dedicated to poets like Denise Levertov, Gary Snyder, Hayden Carruth, and George Seferis, all poets of engagement. His poems testify to the power of sacramental relationships, whether with people he has encountered or with classical masters known only through their texts. Unwilling to eschew the political and social or to cultivate a poetic niche, Hamill's political and social concerns are similarly woven into his work. In the rustic details of "Sheepherder Coffee" "a cup of grounds in my old enameled pot, /then three cups of water and a fire," a consideration of years ago, when "I was happy with my dog, /and cases of books in my funky truck" is complexly intertwined with an wiser knowledge "when I think of that posture now/ I can't help but think/ of Palestinians huddled in their ruins, / the Afghan shepherd with his bleating goats...the Tibetan monk who can't go home," all those "thinking, waiting for whatever comes."

Opening this book at any page, any reader will be richly rewarded. This book,
a lifetime's work, is itself river, mountain, poem.

I Ate The Cosmos For Breakfast, poems by Melissa Studdard
St. Julian Press, Inc.
September 15, 2014
Reviewed by Doug Anderson

Breakfast of the Gods

Melissa Studdard's new book, *I Ate the Cosmos for Breakfast* reminds me of
how C. S. Lewis might have written his Narnia books had he included sex-
uality in his equation of the miraculous. There is no mind/body duality in
Studdard's book: eros is woven into everything. There is no cautious tip-toe-
ing at the edge of the pond but a cannonball splash into the deep end.

The book opens with these lines: "So there God lay, with her
legs splayed,/birthing this screaming world." This is clearly not for the
faint-hearted. In her dedication, "For everyone who has chosen love over
fear," she openly declares her intent. There is no "ironic distance" here; no
hipster detachment, and how refreshing it is.

In "Nirvana," a precise and vital ekphrastic poem about the Re-
medios Varo painting, To Be Reborn, she writes, "Think of trees /poking
branches where/they don't belong," as if life itself is trangressive, as if
order and decorum were uncomfortable illusions pasted onto life to tame
it, and always unsuccessfully. She continues with the human as an unavoid-
able part of this anarchy: "You're/something like that, one/of nature's
great mysteries/thrusting into the narrow rooms/of humanity,/rattling
between the walls/of this synthetic/life, time after time..." Life will be in
spite of fear, Eros will subvert all, Dionysus will win: the rest is pretension.
In a time of extreme political reaction, when politicians are attempting to
reset the country to the nineteen fifties and extremist religion at home and
abroad is attempting to stuff the incubus of change back the bottle with a
kind of slapstick viciousness that would be funny except for the blood, we
have a spontaneously generated voice saying, No, you will not.

In "Where the Gatekeeper Lives," Studdard suggests that we can
unlock both our suffering and "...a cactus" that "bursts with a thousand
golden fruits." Like Beowulf's unlocked word-hoard she celebrates the
irrepressible force that may very well save us in the end, a letting go into the
riptide in order to be borne into a different landscape. There is a childlike
rediscovery of the world, and of sexuality made new. She invites us to
breakfast with delight.

Contributor's Notes

River Allen is studying Creative Writing at the University of Michigan, having previously studied Creative Writing at the University of Wisconsin. Her writing has appeared in The Inside News and Michigan Review. As a contractual Software Engineer, I divide my time between Wisconsin, Colorado, Virginia, and my hometown in Michigan. As always her writing draws upon her rich heritage and her diverse childhood growing up on the shores of Lake Superior.

Doug Anderson's book of poems, The Moon Reflected Fire, won the Kate Tuft's Discovery Award. His book, Blues for Unemployed Secret Police received a grant from The Academy of American Poets. His memoir, Keep Your Head Down, was published by W.W. Norton in 2009. He has taught in the Bennington and Pacific University of Oregon MFA programs, Smith and Emerson Colleges. His work have received awards from The NEA, The Massachusetts Cultural Council, and other funding organizations. He has recent work in Prairie Schoner and work forthcoming in Cimarron Review and Massachusetts Review. He lives in Thorndike, Massachusetts.

Jodi Angel is the author of two collections of short stories. Her first collection, The History of Vegas, was published in 2005 and was named a San Francisco Chronicle Best Book of 2005 as well as a Los Angeles Times Book Review Discovery. Her second collection, You Only Get Letters from Jail, (2013), was named as a Best Book of 2013 by Esquire. Her work has appeared in Esquire, Tin House, One Story, Zoetrope: All-Story, and Byliner, among other publications and anthologies. Her story, "A Good Deuce," was named as a "Distinguished Story" in The Best American Short Stories 2012, and her short story, "Snuff," was selected for inclusion in The Best American Mystery Stories 2014. She lives in Northern California with her wife and daughters.

Jacob M. Appel's first novel, The Man Who Wouldn't Stand Up, won the Dundee International Book Award (2012) and is published by Cargo. Jacob's most recent short story collection, Einstein's Beach House, received the 2013 Pressgang Prize and is published by Butler University. His fiction has appeared in more than two hundred literary journals, including Alaska Quarterly Review, Gettysburg Review and Virginia Quarterly Review. When not writing, Jacob practices medicine in New York City and teaches at the Gotham Writers' Workshop. More at: www.jacobmappel.com

Aleksey Babayev works as a financial engineer in New York, where he lives with his wife and daughter. He draws inspiration from Saturdays, Icelandic landscapes, team sports and Mexican lager. He received his B.A. from Duke University.

Devreaux Baker's awards include the 2014 Barbara Mandigo Kelly Peace Poetry Prize from the Nuclear Age Peace Foundation for her poem, "In The Year Of The Drone", the 2011 PEN Oakland/JosephineMiles Poetry Award, three California Arts Council Grants to produce K-12 original student writing for Public Radio, the Hawaii Council on Humanities International Poetry Prize and the Women's Global Leadership Initiative Poetry Award. She has been nominated for Pushcart prizes and received fellowships to the MacDowell Colony, the Hawthornden Castle, and the Helene Wurlitzer Foundation. She has published four books including; Red Willow People and the recently released book of poems, out of the bones of earth.

JoAnn Balingit's poems appear in Best New Poets, DIAGRAM, Kweli Journal, Verse Daily and elsewhere. She is the author of Words for House Story (2013), two chapbooks, Forage (Wings Press, 2011 Whitebird Chapbook Prize) and Your Heart and How It Works (2010 Global Filipino Literary Award in poetry). She's held fellowships from the Delaware Division of the Arts, VCCA and The Camargo Foundation as a 2014 Bread Loaf Bakeless fellow in fiction. As Delaware's poet laureate, she teaches for schools and nonprofit organizations, and for teens grades 7 – 12 and co-coordinates the Delaware Writing Region of Scholastic Art & Writing Awards. She is an assistant editor at YesYes Books. http://joannbalingit.org

Mason Boyles is a junior at UNC. He has studied fiction at the Kenyon Review writers workshop as well as the Stony Brook writers workshop. His story "Phonebooks" won the Southhampton Review's 2014 fiction prize. His story "Jim Paisley" won Prick of the Spindle's 2014 short fiction prize. Christina M. Castro (Jemez/Taos Pueblo/Chicana) is an educator, writer and community activist. She teaches English at the Institute of American Arts and works as a consultant to the Leadership Institute at the Santa Fe Indian School. Additionally, she teaches Zumba dance fitness, and is constantly engaged in efforts towards indigenous self determination and holistic based social change. She lives in Santa Fe with her husband Baikal and their two children. She thrives best living in her ancestral homelands.

Charles Eagle Bull is from the Pine Ridge Indian Reservation located within the South Dakota borders. He'sa 24 year old Oglala Lakota, carrying heavy dreams of becoming a doctor and returning to his home to make a difference. He started his college career right after high school in 2009 at Oglala Lakota College. There, he studied nursing, life science, natural resources with an emphasis of conservation biology. Finally making the decision to become a doctor, he transferred off to Fort Lewis College to pursue a degree in cellular and molecular biology. This is his first publication.

Chen Chen's work appears/is forthcoming in Poetry, The Massachusetts Review, Narrative, DIAGRAM, [PANK], Tupelo Quarterly, Split This Rock Poem of the Week, The Best American Poetry 2015, among others. A Pushcart Prize nominee, he has received scholarships and fellowships from Kundiman, Tent: Creative Writing, and the Saltonstall Foundation. He is currently finishing an MFA in creative writing at Syracuse University, where he is a University Fellow and a Poetry Editor of Salt Hill. Visit him at chenchenwrites. com. Mark Childress, a native of Alabama, is the author of seven novels: A WORLD MADE OF FIRE, V FOR VICTOR, TENDER, CRAZY IN ALABAMA, GONE FOR GOOD, ONE MISSISSIPPI, and GEORGIA BOTTOMS, as well as screenplays, essays, reviews, reportage, and the libretto for "Georgia Bottoms: A Comic Opera of the Modern South." He lives in Key West, Florida, where he is writing his eighth novel and a film project.

Sandra Cisneros is the founder of the Alfredo Cisneros del Moral Foundation, the Elvira Cisneros Award and the Macondo Foundation, all of which have worked on behalf of creative writers. She is the recipient of numerous awards including a MacArthur. Her writings include novels: THE HOUSE ON MANGO STREET and CARAMELO; short stories: WOMAN HOLLERING CREEK; and poetry collections: MY WICKED WICKED WAYS and LOOSE WOMAN and a children's book, HAIRS. MY WICKED WICKED WAYS will be published in trade paperback and ebook formats in April 2015. She is currently at work on several writing projects including WRITING IN MY PAJAMAS, writing tips; HOW TO BE A CHINGONA, life tips; INFINITO, short stories; CANTOS Y LLANTOS, poems. Her most recent books are a children's book, BRAVO, BRUNO with artist Leslie Greene published in Italy, and HAVE YOU SEEN MARIE?, an illustrated book for adults with artist Ester Hernández, published in the US in October, 2012. In October 2015 she will publish A HOUSE OF MY OWN: STORIES FROM MY LIFE, non-fiction with photographs.

Alfred Corn's eleventh book of poems, titled Unions, appeared in April 2014. He has published a novel, titled Part of His Story; two collections of essays; and a study of prosody. Prizes for his work as a poet include the Guggenheim fellowship, the NEA, an Award in Literature from the Academy of Arts and Letters, and one from the Academy of American Poets. He has taught creative writing at Yale, Columbia, and UCLA. In 2011 Pentameters Theatre in London staged his play Lowell's Bedlam, and in 2013 he was made a Life Fellow of Clare Hall, University of Cambridge, where he worked on a translation of Rilke's Duino Elegies. This past November, Eyewear published his second novel, titled Miranda's Book. Rita Dove is the author of nine poetry collections and several other books. She received the 1987 Pulitzer Prize in poetry and was U.S. Poet Laureate from 1993-95. Among her numerous honors are the National Humanities Medal from President Clinton and the National Medal of Arts from President Obama, making her the only poet with both medals to her credit.

Rita Dove is the author of nine poetry collections and several other books. She received the 1987 Pulitzer Prize in poetry and was U.S. Poet Laureate from 1993-95. Among her numerous honors are the National Humanities Medal from President Clinton and the National Medal of Arts from President Obama, making her the only poet with both medals to her credit.

Anita Endrezze is an author and artist, whose books include at the helm of twilight (Broken Moon Press, 1993), a book of poems which won the Weyerhaeuser-Bumbershoot Award and the Washington State Author's Award and Throwing fire at the Sun, water at the Moon (U of Az Press, 2000): a book about her Yaqui family history told in legends, myths, fiction, and poems. She has published several books of poems in France and England as well as a children's book in Denmark. Her art has appeared on book covers for her own writing and on other national anthologies/literary magazines and for other poets. She has exhibited in WA, England, Wales, Denmark. Media: acrylic paint, collage, colored pencil, watercolor. She has MS and is housebound but tries to remain creative and connected with her artist women friends. They've collaborated on several altered book projects and paintings which have been in museums and galleries. They often donate their work for good causes.

Terri Kirby Erickson is the author of four collections of poetry, including her latest book, A Lake of Light and Clouds (Press 53, 2014); In the Palms of Angels (Press 53, 2011), winner of a Nautilus Book Award; and Telling Tales of Dusk (Press 53, 2009), which was #23 on the 2010 Poetry Foundation Contemporary Best Sellers. Her work appears in the The Writer's Almanac, Ted Kooser's American LifeE, Poetry, Asheville Poetry Review, storySouth, and The Christian Science Monitor, Verse Daily, and her poetry has won multiple awards. She lives in Lewisville, North Carolina. Visit her website at www.terrikirbyerickson.com

Annie Finch's most recent book of poetry is Spells: New and Selected Poems (Wesleyan, 2013). She has recently launched Poetcraft Circles Community (poetcraftcircles.com), a website for poets of all backgrounds excited about exploring form and structure.

Carolyn Forché lives in Maryland and teaches at Georgetown University. Her work focusing on human rights has been widely acclaimed. Among her awards are A Guggenheim Fellowship, The Alice Fay di Castagnola Award and The Lamont Poetry Selection from the Academy of American Poets. Casey Haynes graduated from Western Carolina University, where he interned as Assistant Coordinator for the 2014 Spring Literary Festival and received full scholarships toward attending the Mountain Heritage Literary Festival and Cullowhee Mountain ARTS creative writing workshop. He is currently pursuing his writing between working long hours at a residential home for troubled youth in western Massachusetts.

Joy Harjo has published seven books of poetry, which includes such well-known titles as How We Became Human, New and Selected Poems, W.W. Norton 2004. Her writing awards include a Guggenheim Fellowship, the New Mexico Governor's Award for Excellence in the Arts, the Rasmuson United States Artist Fellowship, and the William Carlos Williams Award from the Poetry Society of America. Her most recent publication is a memoir Crazy Brave, WW Norton 2012, which has won several awards, including the PEN USA Literary Award for Creative Non-Fiction and the American Book Award. She performs with her saxophone nationally and internationally, solo and with her band, the Arrow Dynamics, and tours her one-woman show. She has five CDs of music and poetry including her most recent award-winning album Red Dreams, A Trail Beyond Tears. Her newest collection of poetry, Conflict Resolution for Holy Beings will be published by Norton in Fall 2015, and she is working on her next memoir. She has a commission from the Public Theater of NY to write her musical play, We Were There When Jazz Was Invented, a musical that will restore southeastern natives to the American story of blues and jazz. She lives in Tulsa, Oklahoma.

Linda Hogan (Chickasaw)Former Writer in Residence for The Chickasaw Nation and Professor Emerita from University of Colorado is an internation-ally recognized public speaker and writer of poetry, fiction, and essays. In July, 2014, DARK. SWEET. New and Selected Poems came out from Coffee House Press. Other books include Indios (Wings Press, 2012, long poem, performance) Rounding the Human Corners (Coffee House Press, April 2008, Pulitzer nom-inee) and the well-regarded novel People of the Whale (Norton, August 2008). Her other books include novels Mean Spirit, a winner of the Oklahoma Book Award, the Mountains and Plains Book Award, and a finalist for the Pulitzer Prize; Solar Storms, a finalist for the International Impact Award, and Power, also a finalist for the International Impact Award in Ireland. WW Norton has pub-lished her fiction. In poetry, The Book of Medicines was a finalist for the National Book Critics Circle Award. Her other awards include the Colorado Book Award, Minnesota State Arts Board Grant, an American Book Award, and a Lannan Fellowship from the Lannan Foundation, as NEA Fellowship, a Guggenheim Fellowship and the Lifetime Achievement Award from the Native Writers Circle of the Americas, The Wordcraft Circle, and The Mountains and Plains Booksell-ers Association. Hogan's nonfiction includes Dwellings, A Spiritual History of the Land; and The Woman Who Watches Over the World: A Native Memoir.

In addition, she has, with Brenda Peterson, written Sightings, The Mysterious Journey of the Gray Whale for National Geographic Books, and edited several anthologies on nature and spirituality. She has written the script, Everything Has a Spirit, a PBS documentary on American Indian Religious Freedom. For her writing, Hogan was inducted into the Chickasaw Nation Hall of Fame in 2007.

LeAnne Howe is the author of novels, plays, poetry, screenplays, and scholarship that deal with Native experiences. An enrolled citizen of the Choctaw Nation of Oklahoma, her first novel Shell Shaker, received an American Book Award from the Before Columbus Foundation 2002; Evidence of Red, poetry, won the Oklahoma Book Award, 2006, and Choctalking on Other Realities, memoir, won the 2014 MLA Prize for Studies in Native American Literatures, Cultures, and Languages. Other awards include a Fulbright scholarship 2010-2011; 2012 Lifetime Achievement Award from the Native Writers Circle of the Americas; and a 2012 United States Artists Ford Fellowship. Howe's current project is a new play co-authored with playwright and actress Monique Mojica titled, Sideshow Freaks and Circus Injuns, and a novel, Memoir of a Choctaw in the Arab Revolts, 1917 & 2011. She is the Eidson Distinguished Professor of American Literature at the University of Georgia. For more information see: https://www.youtube.com/watch?v=gWDVttYrMJo&feature=youtu.be

T.R. Hummer's 12th book of poems, Eon, is forthcoming from LSU Press. Skandalon, also from LSU, appeared in 2014. He lives and teaches in Phoenix, AZ, where he is known also to blow a mean sax.

Patricia Spears Jones is an African-American poet, playwright and cultural activist whose new collection, A Lucent Fire: New and Selected Poems will come out in fall 2015 from White Pine Press. In 2014, Living in the Love Economy (Overpass Books) joined her three full-length collections The Weather That Kills (Coffee House); Femme du Monde and Painkiller (Tia Chucha Press) and three other chapbooks. Poems are anthologized in Angles of Ascent: The Norton Anthology of Contemporary African American Poetry; broken land: Poems of Brooklyn, Best American Poetry and elsewhere. Her plays were produced by Mabou Mines. Her articles, essays and interviews are in BOMB, The Poetry Project Newsletter, www.tribes.org, The Black Scholar, and for Harriet, the blog of The Poetry Foundation. She curates and hosts WORDS SUNDAY, a literary series in Brooklyn. She is a senior fellow for the Black Earth Institute, a progressive think tank. Her website is www.psjones.com.

Thomas Johnson was born in Shiprock, New Mexico located in the Navajo Reservation. He graduated from Fort Lewis College, where he studied creative writing. His Navajo culture and heritage are an important theme in his writing and his inspiration includes Sherman Alexie, Leslie Marmon Silko and Joy Harjo. This is his first published work.

Marilyn Kallet is the author of 16 books including The Love That Moves Me, poetry by Black Widow Press. She has also translated Paul Eluard's Last Love Poems (Derniers poèmes d'amour), Benjamin Péret's The Big Game (Le grand jeu), and with Darren Jackson and J. Bradford Anderson has co-translated Chantal Bizzini's Disenchanted City (La Vie Désenchantée), due out in 2015. Kallet directs the Creative Writing Program at the University of Tennessee, where she is Nancy Moore Goslee Professor of English. Each spring she leads poetry workshops for the Virginia Center for the Creative Arts in Auvillar, France.

Clarence Major's most recent collection is From Now On: New and Selected Poems 1970-2015 (University of Georgia Press) 2015. His 1988 novel, Painted Turtle: Woman with Guitar, a New York Times Book Review Notable Book of The Year, was recently reissued by The University of New Mexico Press.

Bobbie Ann Mason is the author of the widely anthologized story "Shiloh," first published in the New Yorker in 1980. She has written several collections of short stories and four novels. Her memoir, Clear Springs, was a finalist for the Pulitzer Prize, and the novel In Country was filmed by Norman Jewison. Her most recent novel is The Girl in the Blue Beret. She has been writer-in-residence at the University of Kentucky.

Bryce Milligan is an award-winning author of children's books, young adult novels, poetry and criticism. Bloomsbury Review calls him a "literary wizard." Publisher, editor and book designer of Wings Press, Bryce has published some 200 books with a focus on multicultural literature, whose authors hail from all over the Americas (half a dozen are state poets laureate). Milligan has authored six poetry collections, including Alms for Oblivion (London: Aark Arts, 2003). He received the Gemini Ink "Award for Literary Excellence" and the St. Mary's University President's Peace Commission's "Art of Peace Award" for "creating work that enhances human understanding through the arts."

Marilyn Nelson's books include The Homeplace; The Fields of Praise; Carver; Fortune's Bones; A Wreath for Emmett Till; Faster than Light, and How I Discovered Poetry. Forthcoming are Seneca Village (Namelos) and American Ace (Penguin/Dial). The 2012 recipient of the Robert Frost Medal and a 2014 recipient of the Furious Flower Lifetime Achievement Award, she was Poet Laureate of CT for five years and founder/director of "Soul Mountain Retreat" for ten. At the present time she is a Chancellor of the

Academy of American Poets and Poet-in-Residence of The Poets Corner at the Cathedral of St. John the Divine.

Susan Power is an enrolled member of the Standing Rock Sioux nation. She is the author of three books, The Grass Dancer, Roofwalker, and Sacred Wilderness. She currently lives in St. Paul, Minnesota.

William Pitt Root has two recent collections from Wings Press: STRANGE ANGELS: New and SUBLIME BLUE: Early Odes of Pablo Neruda, Works by Root have been translated into over 20 languages, and appear here in New Yorker, Atlantic, and Poetry. He lives in Colorado and Arizona with various 4-leggeds-- SadieKat, Zazu, and Mojo Buffalo Buddy.

Rebecca Seiferle's fourth poetry collection, Wild Tongue, (Copper Canyon Press, 2007) won the 2008 Grub Street National Poetry Prize. In 2004 she was awarded a Lannan Foundation Fellowship. She is also a noted translator; Copper Canyon Press published her translation of Vallejo's The Black Heralds in 2003. In 2012, she was named Tucson Poet Laureate.

Kim Shuck (Tsalagi and Goral) writes from a hill in San Francisco where five generations of her family have lived. She is coastal California in the 1960s and Oklahoma lead and zinc mines flavored with pre-colonial Georgia and the Tatra mountains. She has an MFA in fine arts from San Francisco State University. Shuck's writing appears in three books, one chapbook and in many anthologies, magazines, blogs and webzines. Her family is a loose affiliation of judges, bootleggers, goat herders, teachers, Avon ladies, electronic engineers, housekeepers and soldiers. Coming from a group that has done everything everywhere Kim chose to be a storyteller. Her latest book is Clouds Running In, Taurean Horn Press 2014.

Hope Maxwell Snyder was born in Bogotá, Colombia and received an MA in Latin American Literature from Johns Hopkins and a Ph.D. in Spanish Medieval Literature from the University of Manchester. Her poetry has appeared in Alehouse Press, Blackbird, The Comstock Review, The Gettysburg Review, The Kenyon Review, and other journals. Currently on the staff for Bread Loaf in Sicily, Hope also coordinates The Gettysburg Review's Conference for Writers. In the spring of 2015 she'll be at Hood College in Frederick, Maryland, as Writer in Residence.

Barbara Tran's poetry collection, In the Mynah Bird's Own Words, won the Tupelo Press Chapbook Award. Barbara's poems have appeared in The Women's Review of Books, Ploughshares, and The New Yorker. She will be in residence at Hedgebrook this September.

Quincy Troupe edits Black Renaissance Noire at New York University.

He is the author of 20 books, including 10 volumes of poetry and three children's books. His awards include the Paterson Award for Sustained Literary Achievement, the Milt Kessler Poetry Award, three American Book Awards, the Gwendolyn Brooks Poetry Award and a Lifetime Achievement Award from Furious Flowers. His work has been translated into over 30 languages. Troupe's latest book of poems is Errançities (2012) and he is finishing 2 new books of poems, Seduction and Ghost voices. Mr. Troupe is co-author with Miles Davis of Miles: the Autobiography, Earl the Pearl with Earl Monroe and The Pursuit of Happyness, with Chris Gardner. He is also the author of Miles and me, a memoir of his friendship with Miles Davis, soon to be a major motion picture. He lives in Harlem, New York. with his wife, Margaret.

Dan Vera is a writer, editor, and literary historian in Washington, DC. His poetry appears in Speaking Wiri Wiri (Red Hen) and The Space Between Our Danger and Delight (Beothuk) as well as various journals and anthologies. He's the poetry editor for Origins Journal, co-curates the literary history site DC Writers' Homes, and chairs the board of Split This Rock Poetry.

Michael Wasson is nimíipuu from the Nez Perce Reservation and lives in Satomachi, Japan. He was Cutthroat's 2014 Discovery Poet. Recent poems will appear in Poetry Kanto and Waxwing Journal.

Dr Lizzy Welby teaches at the College Fançais Bilingue de Londres. She is an elected Council Member of The Kipling Society and has edited, with an introduction, Rudyard Kipling: Selected Verse (CRW Publishing, 2012). She has published articles on Rudyard Kipling, Angela Carter and Sylvia Plath. She was awarded third prize at the Bridport Prize for Short Fiction in 2012 for a story entitled 'Jugged Hare'. She is the author of Rudyard Kipling's Fiction: Mapping Psychic Spaces Edinburgh Critical Studies in Victorian Culture (Edinburgh: Edinburgh University Press, 2015) and is currently working on a study of Ernest Hemingway's short fiction. Lizzy lives in London with her French partner and their four children. Website: https://eastanglia.academia.edu/LizzyWelby

Linda Weaselhead is the mother of five children, 20 grandchildren and 7 great grandchildren. She is married to Keith (Keon) Weasel Head and they have shared an adventurous 32 years together. She comes from the Bitterroot Salish people of Montana and from Norwegian ancestry. As a student at the University of Montana, she took a creative class taught by Joy Harjo in Native American Literature. At the urging of the students, Joy read one of her poems. Linda was struck with the power, the space, the teaching and the awakening of a force so powerful it has never left her spirit. This duende, as described and defined by Fedrico Garcia Lorca, enhanced Linda's outlook; she always enjoyed life's opportunities despite challenges, as she has been witness to its endless possibilities, edginess and golden moments.

Bill Wetzel is Amskapi Pikuni aka Blackfeet from Montana. He's a former bull rider/wrestler turned writer/obscure tweeter. His work has appeared in the American Indian Culture & Research Journal, Yellow Medicine Review, Studies In Indian Literatures (SAIL), Hinchas de Poesia, Red Ink Magazine, Literary Orphans, the "Best Of Literary Orphans: The Greater Secrets," and "Off The Path: An Anthology of 21st Century American Indian Writers Vol.2." He's a co-founder of Indigipress, and the founder/curator for the Stjukshon Indigenous reading series at Casa Libre en la Solana in Tucson, AZ. In his spare time, he skins together stories and dreams winter against a world of silent legends.

Tanaya Winder is a writer, educator, and motivational speaker from the Southern Ute, Duckwater Shoshone, and Pyramid Lake Paiute Nations. She has a BA an MFA in creative writing from the University of New Mexico. She serves as the editor-in-chief of As/Us: A Space for Women of the World, a literary magazine publishing works by Indigenous women and women of color. A winner of the 2010 A Room Of Her Own Foundation's Orlando prize in poetry, Tanaya's work has appeared or is forthcoming in Superstition Review, Drunkenboat, and Cutthroat. Poems from her manuscript "Love in a Time of Blood Quantum" were produced and performed by Poetic Theater Productions Presents in NYC. She blogs at Letters From A Young Poet http://tanayawinder.wordpress.com/

Elizabeth A. Woody (Navajo/Warm Springs/Wasco/Yakama) is an alumna of the W.K Kellogg Foundation's Fellowship through the AIO Ambassadors program. From 1996-2008 she worked at Ecotrust and designed the Indigenous Leadership program. In 2005-07 she served on the Ford Foundation's advisory council to explore the feasibility of a arts centered foundation for Native Americans. The Native Arts and Cultures Foundation (NACF) incorporated in the fall of 2007 and Elizabeth is founding secretary. Presently she works a Program Officer at Meyer Memorial Trust located in Portland, OR.

2015 Lorain Hemingway Short Story Competition

$2,500 Awaits Winners of 2015 Lorian Hemingway Short Story Competition

• Writers of short fiction are encouraged to enter the 2015 Lorian Hemingway Short Story Competition. The competition has a thirty-one year history of literary excellence, and its organizers are dedicated to enthusiastically supporting the efforts and talent of emerging writers of short fiction whose voices have yet to be heard. Lorian Hemingway, granddaughter of Nobel laureate Ernest Hemingway, is the author of three critically acclaimed books: Walking into the River, Walk on Water, and A World Turned Over. Ms. Hemingway is the competition's final judge.

Prizes and Publication:
• The first-place winner will receive $1,500 and publication of his or her winningstory in Cutthroat: A Journal of the Arts. The second – and third-place winners will receive $500 each. Honorable mentions will also be awarded to entrants whose work demonstrates promise. Cutthroat: A Journal of the Arts was founded by EditorIn-Chief Pamela Uschuk,Vwinner of the 2010 American Book Award for her book Crazy Love, and by poet William Pitt Root, Guggenheim Fellow and NEA recipient. The journal contains some of the finest contemporary fiction and poetry in print, and the Lorian Hemingway Short Story Competition is both proud and grateful to be associated with such a reputable publication.

Eligibility requirements for our 2012 competition are as follows:
What to submit:
• Stories must be original unpublished fiction, typed and double-spaced, and may not exceed 3,500 words in length. We have extended our word limit for the first time in thirty years to 3,500 words rather than 3,000. There are no theme or genre restrictions. Copyright remains property of the author.
Who may submit:
• The literary competition is open to all U.S. and international writers whose fiction has not appeared in a nationally distributed publication with a circulation of 5,000 or more. Writers who have been published by an online magazine or who have selfpublished will be considered on an individual basis.

Submission requirements:
• Submissions may be sent via regular mail or submitted online. Please visit our online submissions page for complete instructions regarding online submissions. Writers may submit multiple entries, but each must be accompanied by an entry fee and separate cover sheet. We do accept simultaneous submissions; however, the writer must notify us if a story is accepted for publication or wins an award prior to our July announcements. No entry confirmation will be given unless requested. No SASE is required.
• The author's name should not appear on the story. Our entrants are judged anonymously. Each story must be accompanied by a separate cover sheet with the writer's name, complete mailing address, e-mail address, phone number, the title of the piece, and the word count. Manuscripts will not be returned. These requirements apply for online submissions as well.

Deadlines and Entry Fees:
• The entry fee is $15 for each story postmarked by May 1, 2014. The late entry fee is $20 for each story postmarked by May 15, 2014. We encourage you to enter by May 1 if at all possible, but please know that your story will still be accepted if you meet the later deadline. Entries postmarked after May 15, 2014 will not be accepted. Entries submitted online after May 15, 2014 will not be accepted. Writers may submit for the 2015 competition beginning May 16, 2014

How to pay your entry fee:
• Entry fees submitted by mail with their accompanying stories may be paid -- in U.S. funds -- via a personal check, cashier's check, or money order. Please make checks payable to LHSSC or The Lorian Hemingway Short Story Competition. Entry fees for online submissions may be paid with PayPal.

Announcement of Winners and Honorable Mentions:
• Winners of the 2014 competition will be announced at the end of July 2014 in Key West, Florida, and posted on our website soon afterward. Only the first-place entrant will be notified personally. All entrants will receive a letter from Lorian Hemingway and a list of winners, either via regular mail or e-mail, by October 1, 2014. All manuscripts and their accompanying entry fees should be sent to The Lorian Hemingway Short Story Competition, P.O. Box 993, Key West, FL 33041 or submitted online. For more information, please explore our website at: http://www. shortstorycompetition. com/ or e-mail: shortstorykw@gmail.com

CPSIA information can be obtained
at www.ICGtesting.com
Printed in the USA
LVHW042106151222
735309LV00003B/460